GI
feel
good

Meals
made easy

GI feel good

Meals
made easy

John Ratcliffe Dip. TCM, Grad Dip Psy
and **Chérie Van Styn** BN

HINKLER
BOOKS

HINKLER
BOOKS

GI Feel Good: Meals Made Easy
Published in 2005 by Hinkler Books Pty Ltd
17–23 Redwood Drive
Dingley VIC 3172 Australia
www.hinklerbooks.com

Previously published as *Meals Made Easy* by Better Healing Solutions in 2004.
ISBN 1 7412 1900 0

Cover Design: Sam Grimmer
Typesetting: Midland Typesetters, Maryborough, Victoria
Printed and bound in Australia

This book is intended as a reference guide only. The information presented here is
designed to help you make informed choices about your health. It is not intended as
a substitute for any treatment or weight loss program prescribed by your doctor.

Contents

Introduction

I am very happy to present our new cookbook. I have burnt the midnight oil, working hard putting together some exciting meal ideas. The in-house test pilot, Dr John, has once again strapped himself in and taken each recipe for a whirl, munching his way diligently through every recipe in this book, as I have watched on, waiting for the customary wry smile or thumbs up for each new creation. It's great to have such a devoted fan.

I have set out to create the best-tasting, easiest to make low GI recipes ever. Often readers have commented that some of the recipes can be a bit involved for everyday use, so I decided to make a collection of recipes that are quick and easy, budget conscious, suitable to take to work and designed for households of two, with some vegatarian dishes. All the meal solutions in this book follow the *GI Feel Good: Health and Weight Loss* formula.

The ingredients used in this book are also easily purchased from your local supermarket or delicatessen. Please make sure that you read the labels when buying canned or pre-packaged products to avoid purchasing products with added sugar. Pre-packaged liquid and dried stock is an example of this. I have included some basic stock recipes for you to follow.

Many of the recipes in this book call for added salt – this enhances flavour when you are not using sugar. Salt is an important compound for the body, however people on a salt-reduced diet for high blood pressure, cardiac disease or other problems should rethink or eliminate the salt used in their cooking as per their doctor or dietician's instructions.

If you are planning on modifying or changing the recipes to suit your personal preferences, please consult the *GI Feel Good: Healthy Shopper's Glycemic Index Pocket Guide* before adding ingredients. This way you won't accidentally combine moderate GI carbohydrates with proteins and fats, or add high GI carbohydrates to your food. Please note that the quantities used in the recipes are specifically designed for following Dr John's formula; don't just add extra cream or more nuts to the meal as this will cause your weight loss to plateau and prevent you from achieving your health goals.

There is plenty of variety and choice available in this recipe book and from the *GI Feel Good: Health and Weight Loss* recipes; you should easily be able to create a menu from these resources. I have also included two meal planners; the 'Quick and Easy Meal Planner' and the 'Vegetarian Meal Planner'.

I am always fond of trying out new ingredients; their smell, taste, texture and appropriate cooking technique. Sometimes my experimentation is a success, sometimes the end result sits in the back of the freezer for months before I finally throw it out. All the recipes in this book are the successes, so don't be afraid to try out new ingredients that are suggested that maybe you haven't used before.

All the recipes are labelled as either carbohydrate or protein; this is so you can decide on a meal-by-meal basis the food type you will be eating. You will also be able to easily identify that having just eaten a carbohydrate-style meal you should wait three hours before eating a protein-style meal; or having just eaten a protein-style meal you should wait five hours before eating a carbohydrate-style meal. Remember to always eat moderate carbohydrates in moderation.

Plan ahead to succeed. Remember the five P's – Proper Preparation Prevents Poor Performance. Be ready for the days when you come home from work too late and too tired to cook. Plan for this scenario and have meals already cooked in the fridge, ready to simply reheat and eat.

Please make full use of our website: www.glycemic-index.com. The forum is a great place to ask questions and get support from other people following this way of eating, while our subscription area offers all types of interactive material and information to help you.

I wish you all the best in your pursuit of good health. I hope you enjoy the food ideas in this book as much as John and I have enjoyed the end results.

Chérie Van Styn

Melbourne 2004

Recipes

Basic Recipes, Snacks and Tips

Chicken stock

Protein

2 kg (4½ lb) chicken bones

2 white onions and skins, finely chopped

3 sticks celery and leaves, chopped

1 cup parsley and stalks, chopped

3 bay leaves

4 stems rosemary

10 black peppercorns

3 litres water

1 tablespoon salt

Place chicken bones and onion in a baking dish and bake 50 minutes at 180°C (350°F). Add chicken bones, onion and all other ingredients to a large saucepan. Bring to the boil; reduce heat and simmer gently for 3 hours, skimming any sediment off the top. Strain stock and discard solids. Keep refrigerated.

Makes approximately: 1½ litres (6 cups) of stock
Total cooking time: 15 minutes preparation, 4 hours cooking

Vegetable stock
Carbohydrate/protein

2 white onions and skins, finely chopped

8 whole spring onions, finely chopped

1 cup parsley and stalks, chopped

4 stems of rosemary

3 sticks celery and leaves, chopped

3 bay leaves

10 black peppercorns

½ small red chilli, seeded and chopped (optional)

Any of the following if available, chopped roughly (save
   your kitchen scraps):

- broccoli stems
- cabbage outer leaves
- cauliflower stems and leaves
- leftover zucchini

2½ litres (10 cups) water

1 tablespoon salt

*Place all ingredients in a large saucepan, cover, bring to the boil,
reduce heat and simmer gently for 1½ hours. Strain off liquid
discarding solids. Keep refrigerated.*

Makes approximately: 1½ (6 cups) litres of stock
Total cooking time: 15 minutes preparation, 1½ hours cooking

Beef stock
Protein

2 kg (4½ lb) beef or veal bones

3 litres (12 cups) water

1 onion, coarsely chopped

2 sticks of celery, chopped

½ bunch fresh parsley

1 teaspoon whole black peppercorns

4 garlic cloves, halved

1 bay leaf

2 cloves

2 tablespoons fresh thyme

1 tablespoon salt

Place bones on a baking tray and bake for 30 minutes at 200°C (390°F), turning once. Place bones and all other ingredients in a large saucepan. Cover, then bring to the boil; reduce heat and allow to simmer for 4 hours. Strain stock, discarding the solids. Keep refrigerated.

Makes: 2 litres (8 cups) of beef stock
Total cooking time: 4½ hours cooking

Fish stock

Protein

1 kg (2 lb) fish bones, heads, tails, prawn shells

1 onion, finely chopped

2 sticks celery, sliced

1 teaspoon salt

1 teaspoon cracked black pepper

3 stems fresh rosemary

½ cup fresh basil, chopped

2½ litres (10 cups) water

Add all ingredients into a large saucepan; cover; bring to the boil; reduce heat and simmer on low for 1 hour. Strain to remove all solid material.

Makes approximately: 1½ litres (6 cups) of fish stock
Total cooking time:15 minutes preparation, 1 hour cooking

Beverages

Fruit juice: Carbohydrate

Remember the same time window rules apply to beverages so drink your juice with your carbohydrate meals only. Juice is a moderate carbohydrate so remember to have moderate carbohydrates in moderation. Only drink juice clearly labelled as having no added sugar, or make your own. Apple juice, orange juice and grapefruit juice are all acceptable. See an example of fruit juice in the following pages.

Vegetable juice: Carbohydrate or Carbohydrate/Protein

When juicing vegetables use only moderate and good carbohydrate vegetables. Moderate carbohydrate vegetables, such as sweet potato, will make juices that you should only drink with carbohydrate meals. Good carbohydrate vegetables such as tomato and celery will make juices that you can drink with either a carbohydrate or a protein meal. See examples of vegetable juice in the following pages.

Tea: Carbohydrate/Protein

Only use tea that is caffeine-free. We use a brand called 'Madura' which is 97% caffeine-free. This is acceptable. Please note that green tea, like most black tea, does have caffeine. You can use a little soymilk in your tea but do not add sugar. See the section on artificial sweeteners if you are thinking about adding them to your tea.

Herbal tea: Carbohydrate/Protein

Most herbal teas are caffeine-free and therefore suitable to have with any meal. Some suggested herbal teas include lemon, peppermint and camomile. Avoid the fruit flavoured and liquorice root teas as they may cause your weight to plateau. See the section on artificial sweeteners if you are thinking about adding them to your herbal tea.

Coffee: Carbohydrate/Protein

Use decaffeinated coffee only. You can use a little soymilk in your decaffeinated coffee but do not add any sugar. See the section on artificial sweeteners if you are thinking about adding them to your decaffeinated coffee.

Soymilk: Carbohydrate

Soymilk is the alternative to regular milk. Made from soy beans it is classified as a moderate carbohydrate, however adding a small amount to your tea and coffee is alright and shouldn't cause you any problems. Choose sugar-free soymilk that does not contain maltodextrine. Try to avoid drinking straight soymilk; being a moderate carbohydrate you should only use it in moderation. Some on your muesli in the morning and in your cups of tea should be fine.

Milk: Carbohydrate/Lipid

Milk is not allowed because it is a combination of sugar and fat and, from experience, guaranteed to hold up your progress. Excellent alternative sources of calcium are Parmesan cheese, canned salmon with bones and white beans, while spinach, broccoli, bok choy and soy beans also contribute to your recommended daily intake of calcium.

Beverages you should forget about are: cola drinks, soft drinks, milk drinks, goat's milk, sheep's milk, rice milk, cordial, sports drinks, flavoured yoghurt drinks, wine, beer, spirits, regular coffee and energy drinks.

Beverages you should become reacquainted with:

     – WATER

     – WATER

     – WATER

Water is the most thirst-quenching substance known. You can drink water with any meal and at any time of the day. You should have at least 6–8 glasses of water per day (NB: Cups of tea and decaffeinated coffee will also count towards your water intake tally.)

Fruit
Carbohydrate

Fruit is generally a moderate carbohydrate and therefore should be eaten in moderation. Remember to observe the time intervals between eating a carbohydrate meal and a protein meal when eating fruit.

Fruit that can be eaten in moderation include:

- Apples
- Dried apples
- Oranges
- Grapefruit
- Apricots
- Dried apricots
- Cherries
- Peaches
- Pears
- Plums
- Rhubarb
- Strawberries

Fruit that you should avoid include:

- Bananas
- Kiwi fruit
- Mango
- Paw paw
- Pineapple
- Rockmelon
- Watermelon
- Raisins
- Sultanas
- Currants

- Grapes
- Figs
- Dates.

Examples of serves of fruit include:

- 1 handful of dried apricots *or*
- 140g (4½ oz) of diced pears in natural juice *or*
- 1 orange *or*
- 6 strawberries

Fresh vegetables
Carbohydrate/Protein

You can make a quick and easy low GI snack using good carbo-hydrate vegetables. These vegetables will have a GI of less than 20 and can be eaten with either protein- or carbohydrate-style meals or between meals. Fresh vegetables are a good source of fibre and nutrients. Fresh vegetables that you can eat include:

- Tomato
- Celery
- Cucumber
- Mushroom
- Capsicum
- Zucchini
- Fennel

See suggestion for vegetable crudités you can make to serve with dips on the next page.

Vegetable crudités

Carbohydrate/Protein

½ stick of celery, cut into matchsticks

4 small button mushrooms

4 grape tomatoes

Makes vegetable crudités to serve with dips.

Serves: 2

Total cooking time: 5 minutes preparation

Nuts
Protein

The following nuts have a GI of zero (or an undetectable GI); they are therefore classified as a protein meal. These nuts are pecans, walnuts, brazil nuts, macadamias, almonds and hazelnuts. Although these nuts have a zero GI some people have found that they reached a plateau in their weight loss when eating too many nuts, particularly when eating macadamias and almonds. If you find your weight loss plateaus when including these nuts in your diet, then either decrease the quantity you are eating or remove them from your diet. We recommend no more than 5–6 nuts as an individual snack serving once per day.

Cheese and sliced/cured meats

Protein

Cheese is classified as a protein. You can eat cheese with any protein meal and between protein meals, such as for morning or afternoon tea. The only cheese not suitable is any cheese made with goat's milk or any cheese containing fruit, nuts or poppy seeds. You should also eat soft white cheeses in moderation and use mascarpone cheese with caution. Hard yellow cheese you are free to enjoy.

Sliced/cured meats are also a good snack which can be eaten with cheese. You can eat meats with any protein meal or between protein meals. Some sliced/cured meats will have sugar as an ingredient on the packaging; this is because the meat is cured using a mixture of sugar and salt. You will notice that sugar features low on the list of ingredients. You can still eat this meat as a protein. Other sliced/cured meats use sugar as an ingredient mixed with the meat product during processing; these may cause your weight loss to plateau. When selecting sliced/cured meat you should read the nutritional panel on the product. You should look for a sugar content of less than 1g per 100g serving. If you are unsure, or you have reached a plateau in your weight loss then try leaving the sliced/cured meat out of your diet.

An example of a serve of cheese:
- 2 slices of cheddar cheese

Examples of serves of sliced or cured meat:
- 1 slice of roasted turkey breast *or*
- 3 slices of pepperoni

Chickpea dip
Carbohydrate

800g (28 oz) canned chickpeas, rinsed and drained

Juice of 1 lemon

3 garlic cloves, crushed

1 tablespoon fresh flat-leaf parsley leaves, chopped

1 tablespoon fresh mint leaves, chopped

Sea salt and freshly cracked black pepper to taste

In a processor puree chickpeas, then combine with lemon juice, garlic, parsley, mint and seasoning. Serve with fresh vegetables or with carbohydrate-style meals.

Makes: 2 cups of dip
Total cooking time: 5 minutes preparation

Guacamole

Protein

1 small red onion, finely diced

1 long green chilli, finely chopped

Juice of 1 lime

3 avocadoes, mashed

Sea salt and freshly cracked black pepper to taste

Combine all ingredients together and serve with vegetable crudités or with protein-style meals.

Makes: 2 cups of dip
Total cooking time: 5 minutes preparation

Smoked salmon dip

Protein

100g (3½ oz) smoked salmon

Juice of ½ lemon

1 cup ricotta cheese

Sea salt to taste

In a blender process salmon, lemon juice and ricotta. Season to taste. Serve with fresh vegetables or protein-style meal.

Makes: 1½ cups dip
Total cooking time: 5 minutes preparation

Quick and easy

Egg and bacon pies

Muesli with apricots, mandarin and vanilla

Salmon steaks served on asparagus with fresh dill dressing

Fresh pasta with tomato passata, sun-dried tomatoes and oregano

Beef medallions with zucchini, caper and lemon salad

*Stir-fried prawns, beans and bok choy with ginger and
kaffir lime leaves*

*Zucchini and smoked salmon frittata with snipped chives and
fresh dill*

Creamy Asian chicken soup

*Lemon and garlic lamb cutlets served with witlof, mint and
walnut salad*

Quick minestrone

Vegetable kebabs with Cajun spices and tomato salsa

Spicy roasted baby snapper served with garlic and sage spinach

Chicken Caesar salad

Sardines and tomatoes with caper and parsley dressing

Roast pork stir-fry with coriander and Chinese five spice

Pepper beef and blue cheese salad with fresh parsley and chive dressing

*Spicy fish fillets with tomato salsa served with garlic and
chilli broccolini*

*Kangaroo fillets with creamy tarragon and caper mayonnaise and
rocket salad*

Creamy fish soup with fresh chives

Chilli pork chops served with harissa and sumac spiced spinach

Scrambled eggs with garlic mushrooms and grilled pancetta

*Tuna with ginger, chilli and lemongrass drizzled with
wasabi dressing*

Chicken braised with spices
Lamb with thyme and garlic served with fresh tomato and
bocconcini salad
Chilli octopus and calamari salad

Egg and bacon pies

Protein

1 tablespoon butter

4 bacon rashers, finely chopped

500g (16 oz) ricotta cheese

2 eggs

¾ cup mozzarella cheese

¼ cup grated Parmesan cheese.

Heat butter in a frying pan, add bacon and cook for 3 minutes. Combine bacon, ricotta, egg, mozzarella and Parmesan cheese in a food processor. Spoon mixture into 8 greased muffin tins. Bake at 180°C (350°F) for 30 minutes.

Makes: 8 muffins
Total cooking time: 5 minutes preparation, 30 minutes cooking

Muesli with apricots, mandarin and vanilla

Carbohydrate

Rind of ½ mandarin, finely chopped

700g (23 oz) rolled oats

100g (3½ oz) processed bran

60g (2 oz) coarse oatmeal

200g (7 oz) dried apricots, diced

1 vanilla bean pod

Place mandarin rind on a plate and microwave on high for 30 seconds. Allow to cool before combining all ingredients together. Cover and allow to stand for 24 hours before using. Retain and reuse vanilla bean pod when muesli is finished. Use soymilk with your muesli and top with fruit such as fresh strawberries, apricots or pear.

Makes: 10 bowls
Total cooking time: 5 minutes preparation

Salmon steaks served on asparagus with fresh dill dressing

Protein

Salmon steaks

1 tablespoon olive oil

4 salmon steaks

16 asparagus spears, trimmed

Sea salt and freshly ground black pepper to taste

Dill dressing

2 tablespoons cream

1 teaspoon lemon juice

1 tablespoon white wine vinegar

2 tablespoons fresh dill sprigs, finely chopped

Sea salt and freshly cracked black pepper to taste

Sprigs of fresh dill, extra to garnish

Heat oil in a large frying pan, season the salmon, then cook for 3–4 minutes each side or until just cooked through.

In a saucepan of boiling salted water, cook the asparagus until just tender; drain. Serve salmon on top of asparagus spears.

For the dressing, whisk together cream, lemon juice, vinegar, dill and seasoning. Spoon dressing over the salmon and asparagus and garnish with sprigs of fresh dill.

Serves: 4

Total cooking time: 5 minutes preparation, 8 minutes cooking

Fresh pasta with tomato passata, sun-dried tomatoes and oregano

Carbohydrate

Tomato passata is found in the pasta sauce aisle in the supermarket. It is usually in a jar and is simply pureed tomatoes with salt.

600g (20 oz) fresh fettuccine pasta

2 cups tomato passata

10 semi sun-dried tomatoes, chopped

2 tablespoons fresh oregano leaves, chopped

Sea salt and freshly cracked black pepper to taste

Cook pasta in a saucepan of boiling salted water for 3 minutes; drain. Heat tomato passata in a large saucepan, add the pasta, sun-dried tomatoes, oregano and seasoning; toss well to combine and serve.

Serves: 4

Total cooking time: 5 minutes preparation, 5 minutes cooking

Beef medallions with zucchini, caper and lemon salad

Protein

Beef medallions

4 beef round medallions

2 tablespoons walnuts

Zest of 1 lemon

2 tablespoons olive oil

2 tablespoons fresh mint

Sea salt and freshly cracked black pepper to taste

Zucchini, caper and lemon salad

2 green zucchini, cut into thin ribbons with a
    vegetable peeler

1 yellow zucchini, cut into thin ribbons with a
    vegetable peeler

Juice and zest of 1 lemon

3 tablespoons extra virgin olive oil

2 tablespoons fresh oregano, coarsely chopped

1 tablespoon small salted capers

Sea salt and freshly ground black pepper to taste

Combine walnuts, zest, oil, mint and seasoning in a food processor to form a coarse paste. Rub paste into the beef medallions, then grill on a heated oiled barbecue for 3 minutes each side or until cooked as desired.

For the salad, combine lemon juice and zest, oil, oregano and capers and mix well. Pour dressing over zucchini ribbons and season; toss well to combine. Serve beef medallions with salad to the side.

Serves: 4

Total cooking time: 10 minutes preparation, 6 minutes cooking

Stir-fried prawns, beans and bok choy with ginger and kaffir lime leaves

Protein

Kaffir lime leaves (their real name being Makrut lime leaves) and Thai basil are both available in most good fruit and vegetable stores. I have found them hard to come by in super-markets, although I am sure they will be more readily available as people become better acquainted with these wonderful herbs.

2 tablespoons peanut oil

1 teaspoon sesame oil

1 garlic clove, crushed

350g (12 oz) large uncooked prawn meat

4 kaffir lime leaves, finely shredded

1 teaspoon fresh ginger, finely chopped

150g (5 oz) green snake beans, trimmed and cut into
   5 cm (2 inch) lengths

3 baby bok choy, quartered lengthways

Juice of 1 lime

2 teaspoons fish sauce

¼ cup fresh Thai basil leaves, finely chopped

Heat oils in a wok on high heat; add garlic, prawns, lime leaves, ginger, beans and bok choy; stir-fry 5 minutes. Add lime juice and fish sauce and stir-fry a further 2 minutes. Stir through basil leaves and serve.

Serves: 4

Total cooking time: 5 minutes preparation, 8 minutes cooking

Zucchini and smoked salmon frittata with snipped chives and fresh dill

Protein

This recipe is great for breakfast as well as lunch or dinner.

1 tablespoon olive oil

1 medium zucchini, grated

4 eggs, lightly beaten

1 tablespoon cream

2 tablespoons freshly grated Parmesan cheese

Sea salt and freshly ground black pepper to taste

50g (1½ oz) smoked salmon

1 tablespoon sour cream

2 teaspoons fresh chives, snipped

2 teaspoons fresh dill, chopped

Heat oil in a frying pan, add zucchini and fry for 5 minutes. Combine eggs, cream, Parmesan cheese and seasoning; add to zucchini.

Cook zucchini and egg mixture over low heat for 8 minutes or until set. Remove frittata from pan and place on a serving platter. Layer salmon on top of frittata. Combine sour cream, chives, 1 teaspoon of water and seasoning; dollop sour cream mixture on top of salmon and garnish with dill.

Serves: 2
Total cooking time: 5 minutes preparation, 15 minutes cooking

Creamy Asian chicken soup

Protein

2 tablespoons peanut oil

3 chicken breast fillets

1 onion, sliced

1 garlic clove, crushed

4 rashers bacon, chopped

8 button mushrooms, sliced

2 star anise

3 slices of ginger

3 cloves

1 stick of cinnamon

5 cups water

4 tablespoons cream

½ cup fresh coriander leaves, chopped

Sea salt and freshly cracked black pepper to taste

Heat peanut oil in a large frying pan and fry chicken for 3 minutes each side or until cooked through. Remove chicken from pan and allow to rest for 5 minutes before slicing thinly.

To the wok add onion and garlic, then stir-fry until onion softens. Add bacon, mushrooms, star anise, ginger, cloves and cinnamon, then stir-fry 5 minutes. Add chicken and water, then bring to the boil. Reduce heat then add cream and gently re-heat. Stir through coriander and seasoning. Remove ginger slices, cloves, star anise and cinnamon stick before serving.

Serves: 4

Total cooking time: 5 minutes preparation, 15 minutes cooking

Lemon and garlic lamb cutlets served with witlof, mint and walnut salad

Protein

Lemon and garlic lamb cutlets

12 French lamb cutlets

Zest and juice of 1 lemon

2 garlic cloves, crushed

2 tablespoons olive oil

½ teaspoon salt

¼ teaspoon freshly cracked black pepper

Witlof, mint and walnut salad

6 witlof, bases trimmed, leaves separated

2 tablespoons fresh mint, finely chopped

50g (1½ oz) walnuts

100g (3½ oz) feta, crumbled

2 tablespoons walnut oil

Juice of ½ lemon

Combine lemon zest, juice, garlic, oil and seasoning; brush over both sides of the cutlets. Cook cutlets under a preheated grill or on the barbecue for 2–3 minutes each side or until cooked as desired.

For the witlof and mint salad, combine all ingredients and toss well. Serve the lamb cutlets with the salad to the side.

Serves: 4

Total cooking time: 5 minutes preparation, 5 minutes cooking

Quick minestrone
Carbohydrate

5 cups vegetable stock

400g (14 oz) diced tomatoes

2 tablespoons tomato paste

1 can red kidney beans, rinsed and drained

2 cups fresh spiral pasta

1 tablespoon fresh oregano, chopped

2 tablespoons fresh parsley, chopped

Sea salt and freshly cracked black pepper to taste

In a large saucepan combine stock, tomatoes and tomato paste.
Bring to the boil, then add beans and pasta. Simmer for 4 minutes;
stir through herbs and seasoning and serve.

Serve: 4
Total cooking time: 10 minutes

Vegetable kebabs with Cajun spices and tomato salsa

Protein

Lebanese eggplants are thin sausage-shaped eggplants. They are usually available in the supermarket or local fruit and vegetable store.

Vegetable kebabs

12 bamboo skewers,

3 baby yellow squash, cut into wedges

3 Lebanese eggplants, cut into 2 cm (½ inch) slices

1 red capsicum, seeded and cut into wedges

3 zucchinis, cut into 2 cm (½ inch) slices

2 red onions, peeled, ends left intact and cut into wedges

4 tablespoons butter, melted

2 teaspoons dried thyme

2 teaspoons paprika

½ teaspoon salt

¼ teaspoon freshly ground black pepper

Salsa

½ red onion, very finely chopped

1 garlic clove, crushed

1 fresh long red chilli, seeded and finely chopped

6 Roma tomatoes, finely chopped

2 tablespoons fresh coriander, chopped

Juice of 1 lime

Sea salt and freshly ground black pepper to taste

Thread alternating vegetables onto the skewers. Combine butter, thyme, paprika, salt and pepper. Brush skewered vegetables liberally with butter mixture. Cook skewers on a hot barbecue or under a grill for 10 minutes; basting vegetables frequently with spice mixture and turning several times until vegetables are tender and cooked through.

For the salsa, combine all ingredients, toss well and serve with the kebabs.

Serves: 4
Total cooking time: 10 minutes preparation, 10 minutes cooking

Spicy roasted baby snapper served with garlic and sage spinach

Protein

Spicy roasted baby snapper

3 garlic cloves, peeled

2 teaspoons salt

Zest of 1 lemon

2 teaspoons paprika

1 teaspoon chilli powder

1 teaspoon ground cinnamon

3 tablespoons vegetable oil

4 whole baby snapper

1 tablespoon vegetable oil, extra

Garlic and sage spinach

2 tablespoons butter

500g (16 oz) baby English spinach leaves

1 garlic clove, crushed

2 tablespoons fresh sage leaves, shredded

Sea salt and freshly cracked black pepper to taste

2 tablespoons fresh sage leaves, extra to garnish

In a mortar pound garlic, salt, zest, paprika, chilli, cinnamon and oil to form a smooth paste. Make 3 deep cuts on both sides of the snapper; brush snapper all over with the garlic and spice paste. Heat extra vegetable oil in a large frying pan, add the fish and brown well over high heat for 1 minute each side. Transfer fish to a baking tray and cook at 200°C (390°F) for 8 minutes.

For the garlic and sage spinach, melt butter in a large wok, add spinach, garlic, sage and seasoning and stir-fry 5 minutes or until spinach leaves have wilted. Serve spinach onto 4 plates and top with the cooked baby snapper. Garnish with extra sage leaves.

Serves: 4
Total cooking time: 5 minutes preparation, 10 minutes cooking

Chicken Caesar salad

Protein

2 tablespoons olive oil

2 chicken breast fillets

8 thin slices prosciutto

2 baby cos lettuces, separated and washed

10 anchovies

4 eggs, lightly poached so that centres remain soft

⅓ cup Parmesan cheese shavings, to serve

Dressing

2 egg yolks

4 anchovies, extra

4 tablespoons cream

¼ cup white wine vinegar

½ cup olive oil

Sea salt and freshly ground black pepper to taste

Heat oil in a large frying pan, cook chicken 3–4 minutes each side or until golden brown and cooked through. Allow chicken to rest 5 minutes before slicing and setting aside. Grill prosciutto until crisp, break into smaller pieces. Combine sliced chicken, prosciutto, anchovies and cos lettuce. Divide salad between four bowls.

To make the dressing, combine egg yolk, cream, anchovies and vinegar; whisk egg and cream mixture and gradually add olive oil. Season dressing then serve drizzled over the salad. Top each salad with a poached egg and Parmesan cheese shavings.

Serves: 4
Total cooking time: 5 minutes preparation, 12 minutes cooking

Sardines and tomatoes with caper and parsley dressing

Protein

Canned sardines are used in this recipe as the bones are much softer and hardly noticeable when eating this dish. You can try using fresh sardine fillets and barbecuing them if you like, however I must warn you that the bones in the fresh fillets are plentiful and hazardous.

300g (9½ oz) sardine fillets in oil, drained
4 large ripe tomatoes, sliced thickly
1 small red onion, thinly sliced
Sea salt and freshly cracked black pepper to taste

Caper and parsley dressing
2 tablespoons red wine vinegar
4 tablespoons olive oil
1 tablespoon capers, chopped
1 garlic clove, crushed
3 tablespoons fresh flat-leaf parsley, finely chopped

On a heated oiled barbecue cook sardines 1 minute each side. Arrange tomatoes and onion onto four plates, top with the sardines and season.

For the dressing, combine all ingredients, whisk together well, pour over the sardines and serve.

Serves: 4
Total cooking time: 5 minutes preparation, 4 minutes cooking

Roast pork stir-fry with coriander and Chinese five spice

Protein

This recipe is one of John's favourites. Whenever I cook a pork roast I make sure that there will be left-overs to make this recipe the next day, otherwise there would be loud complaints.

1 tablespoon peanut oil

1 teaspoon sesame oil

1 onion, sliced

1 garlic clove, crushed

1 teaspoon fresh ginger, grated

400g (14 oz) roast pork, sliced

12 mushrooms, sliced

10 green snake beans, trimmed and cut into
    5 cm (2 inch) lengths

3 cups wom bok (Chinese cabbage), shredded

2 cups bean shoots

1 teaspoon Chinese five spice powder

½ teaspoon chilli powder, or to taste

Juice of ½ lemon

½ cup coriander leaves

Sea salt and freshly cracked black pepper to taste

Heat oils in a large wok; add onion and garlic and fry until onion softens. Add ginger, pork and mushrooms and stir-fry 3 minutes. Add beans, wom bok, bean shoots, five spice and chilli powder, then stir-fry for 6 minutes. Stir through lemon juice, coriander leaves and seasoning and serve.

Serves: 4

Total cooking time: 5 minutes preparation, 15 minutes cooking

Pepper beef and blue cheese salad with fresh parsley and chive dressing

Protein

Pepper beef and blue cheese salad

4 beef sirloin steaks

4 tablespoons olive oil

Freshly cracked black pepper

150g (5 oz) blue vein cheese, sliced thinly into wedges

3 cups of mixed salad

Parsley and chive dressing

1 garlic clove, crushed

½ cup olive oil

¼ cup white wine vinegar

2 tablespoons fresh flat leaf parsley, chopped

1 tablespoon fresh chives, chopped

Sea salt and freshly cracked black pepper to taste

Brush steaks with oil and season liberally with the pepper. Cook steaks for 3–4 minutes each side or until cooked as desired. Allow steaks to rest for 5 minutes before thinly slicing on the diagonal. Combine beef, mixed salad leaves and cheese.

For the dressing, combine garlic, oil, vinegar, parsley and chives, mix well. Drizzle dressing over the salad, toss well to combine; season and serve.

Serves: 4

Total cooking time: 5 minutes preparation, 15 minutes cooking and resting

Spicy fish fillets with tomato salsa served with garlic and chilli broccolini

Protein

Broccolini looks very similar to normal broccoli. You should be able to find it in your supermarket or local fruit and vegetable store. If you can not find broccolini then substitute a head of broccoli cut into small florets.

Spicy fish fillets

1 teaspoon chilli powder

2 tablespoons dried oregano

1 tablespoon dried thyme

2 teaspoons paprika

1 teaspoon salt

2 tablespoons butter

2 garlic cloves, crushed

4 large white fish fillets of choice

Oregano and tomato salsa

4 tomatoes, seeded, finely chopped

1 red onion, finely chopped

1 tablespoon olive oil

1 tablespoon fresh oregano, finely chopped

Sea salt and freshly ground black pepper to taste

Garlic and chilli broccolini

2 bunches broccolini, trimmed, washed and separated
   lengthways

2 tablespoons olive oil

2 garlic cloves, crushed

1 fresh birds-eye chilli, seeded and finely chopped
Sea salt and freshly ground pepper to taste

Combine chilli, oregano, thyme, paprika and salt. Melt butter in a saucepan, add garlic and sauté for 2 minutes. Baste fish fillets with garlic butter then season with the herb and spice mixture. Cook fish in a large frying pan for 2 minutes each side or until just cooked through.

For the salsa, combine all ingredients and season to taste. Serve salsa over the fish fillets.

For the broccolini, cook broccolini in a saucepan of boiling salted water for 5 minutes; drain. Heat olive oil in a frying pan, add garlic, chilli and broccolini, stir-fry for 3 minutes, season and serve with the fish and salsa.

Serves: 4
Total cooking time: 10 minutes preparation, 10 minutes cooking

Kangaroo fillets with creamy tarragon and caper mayonnaise and rocket salad

Protein

If you have not cooked kangaroo before then be careful not to overcook it. Kangaroo should be quite bloody like a rare steak. If it is cooked any more than this then it tends to become quite tough. The meat will also be more tender if it is 3–4 days old; ask your butcher how old the meat is before you purchase it.

Kangaroo fillets

4 kangaroo fillets

4 tablespoons olive oil

Freshly cracked black pepper

Creamy tarragon and caper mayonnaise

2 egg yolks

1 tablespoon cream

Juice of ½ lemon

½ cup olive oil

1 teaspoon dried tarragon

10 capers

Sea salt and freshly cracked black pepper to taste

Rocket salad

2 tablespoons olive oil

2 tablespoons white wine vinegar

2 cups rocket

Sea salt and freshly cracked black pepper to taste

Brush kangaroo fillets with olive oil then season with pepper. Cook kangaroo on a heated, oiled barbecue for 2 minutes each side or until cooked as desired. Stand in a warm place for 5 minutes before serving.

For the mayonnaise, combine egg yolks, cream and lemon juice; gradually add oil while whisking. Add tarragon, capers and seasoning and process until smooth. Serve mayonnaise drizzled over kangaroo fillets.

For the rocket salad, combine olive oil and vinegar, then pour over the rocket, season, and toss well. Serve rocket salad to the side.

Serves: 4
Total cooking time: 10 minutes preparation, 4 minutes cooking

Creamy fish soup with fresh chives

Protein

600g (20 oz) fish fillets, skin removed, chopped into
   5 cm (2 inch) pieces

12 egg yolks, lightly beaten

Juice of 1 lemon

1½ cups olive oil

1 cup hot fish stock

2 garlic cloves, crushed

2 tablespoons fresh chives, chopped

Sea salt and freshly cracked black pepper to taste

Poach fish in a steamer for 5 minutes or until cooked through, then set aside.

Beat together egg yolks and lemon juice; gradually add olive oil while whisking. Add half the hot fish stock and the garlic and mix well. Place egg mixture over low heat and gently warm, stirring continuously until mixture thicken. Stir through remaining stock, poached fish, chives and seasoning, then serve.

Serves: 4

Total cooking time: 10 minutes preparation, 10 minutes cooking

Chilli pork chops with harissa and sumac spiced spinach

Protein

Harissa is a Middle Eastern spice mix; you will find it at the deli.

Chilli pork chops

2 tablespoons olive oil

2 garlic cloves, crushed

1 teaspoon ground cumin

1 teaspoon ground coriander

1 teaspoon chilli powder

1 teaspoon salt

½ teaspoon freshly ground black pepper

4 pork chops

Harissa and sumac spiced spinach

2 tablespoons butter

400g (14 oz) baby English spinach leaves

2 teaspoons harissa

1 teaspoon sumac

Sea salt and freshly cracked black pepper to taste

Combine oil, garlic, cumin, coriander, chilli, salt and pepper. Brush pork chops with the herb and spice mixture. Cook pork on a heated oiled barbecue 5 minutes each side; while cooking, baste frequently with any remaining herb and spice mixture.

For the spinach, melt butter in a large saucepan, add spinach, harissa, and sumac and stir-fry for 3 minutes or until spinach begins to wilt. Season spinach. Serve pork chops with spinach to the side.

Serves: 4

Total cooking time: 5 minutes preparation, 10 minutes cooking

Scrambled eggs with garlic mushrooms and grilled pancetta

Protein

This is great for a special breakfast feast or even for lunch or dinner. If you can't get some of the mushrooms suggested in the recipe, just substitute them with a combination of different mushroom varieties that you can find.

Scrambled eggs

6 eggs, lightly beaten

2 tablespoons cream

1 tablespoon butter, melted

Sea salt and freshly cracked black pepper to taste

Garlic mushrooms

3 tablespoons butter

2 garlic cloves, crushed

6 button mushrooms, sliced

4 oyster mushrooms, sliced

6 shitake mushrooms, sliced

6 Swiss brown mushrooms, sliced

2 tablespoons fresh flat-leaf parsley, chopped

Sea salt and freshly ground pepper to taste

12 slices of pancetta

Combine eggs, cream, butter and seasoning, whisk together well. Heat a non-stick frying pan; add egg mixture and cook 4 minutes over medium heat stirring frequently.

For the garlic mushrooms, melt butter in a large frying pan, add garlic and cook 30 seconds before adding the mushrooms. Cook mushrooms for about 5 minutes stirring occasionally. Toss through parsley and season.

Grill pancetta 2 minutes each side under a hot grill and serve with the eggs and mushrooms onto 4 plates.

Serves: 4
Total cooking time: 5 minutes preparation, 10 minutes cooking

Tuna with ginger, chilli and lemongrass drizzled with wasabi dressing

Protein

4 tablespoons olive oil

Juice of 1 lemon

2 teaspoons freshly grated ginger

1 red birds-eye chilli, seeded and finely chopped

2 tablespoons fresh finely chopped lemongrass

4 tuna steaks

Sea salt and freshly cracked black pepper to taste

2 tablespoons apple cider vinegar

1 teaspoon wasabi paste, or to taste

4 tablespoons sour cream

3 cups mixed salad leaves

1 tablespoon peanut oil

1 teaspoon sesame oil

½ cucumber, sliced

Combine oil, lemon juice, ginger, chilli and lemongrass, pour marinade over tuna steaks and refrigerate 30 minutes. After marinating, drain tuna and reserve the marinade. Cook tuna on a barbecue for 3 minutes each side, basting frequently with the marinade. Serve onto four plates and season.

For the dressing, combine vinegar, wasabi paste and sour cream; season with salt and drizzle over the tuna.

Combine salad leaves, peanut oil, sesame oil and cucumber; toss well to combine and serve to the side.

Serves: 4

Total cooking time: 10 minutes preparation, 30 minutes cooking

Chicken braised with spices

Protein

3 tablespoons olive oil

2 onions, finely chopped

2 garlic cloves, crushed

2 teaspoons paprika

½ teaspoon cayenne pepper, or to taste

1½ teaspoons ground ginger

1½ teaspoons ground turmeric

500g (16 oz) diced chicken

2 dried bay leaves

2 tablespoons tomato paste

1 can diced tomatoes

¼ cup red wine vinegar

Juice of 1 lemon

½ cup fresh coriander leaves, chopped

Sea salt and freshly cracked black pepper to taste

Heat oil in a large frying pan, add onions and garlic; stir-fry until onions softened, then remove from pan. To the pan add paprika, cayenne pepper, ginger, turmeric, and chicken, stir-fry until chicken is golden brown and cooked through. Add cooked onions, bay leaves, tomato paste, tomatoes, vinegar and lemon juice. Bring to the boil then simmer for 10 minutes, uncovered. Stir through coriander and seasoning, remove bay leaves. Serve chicken with long green beans cooked in boiling salted water; drained and seasoned with salt and pepper and scattered over with fresh, chopped flat-leaf parsley.

Serves: 4

Total cooking time: 5 minutes preparation, 15 minutes cooking

Lamb with thyme and garlic served with fresh tomato and bocconcini salad

Protein

Bocconcini, used in this recipe, is a type of cheese. It should be readily available at your local delicatessen.

Lamb with thyme and garlic

4 lamb backstraps

2 tablespoons fresh thyme, chopped

1 garlic clove, crushed

2 tablespoons olive oil

Sea salt and freshly cracked black pepper to taste

Fresh tomato, bocconcini and basil salad

3 tomatoes, sliced thickly

200g (7 oz) bocconcini, sliced thickly

2 tablespoons basil leaves, chopped

¼ cup olive oil

Sea salt and freshly cracked black pepper to taste

Combine thyme, garlic, oil and seasoning. Baste lamb liberally with the thyme and garlic mixture. Grill lamb on a heated oiled barbecue for 3 minutes each side or until cooked as desired.

For the salad, arrange tomato and bocconcini slices in overlapping, alternating layers onto 4 plates. Combine basil, olive oil and seasoning and drizzle over the salad. Serve lamb with salad to the side.

Serves: 4

Total cooking time: 5 minutes preparation, 6 minutes cooking

Chilli octopus and calamari salad

Protein

4 tablespoons olive oil

500g (16 oz) baby octopus, heads removed

2 calamari hoods, scored and cut into pieces

2 garlic cloves, crushed

½ teaspoon dried chilli flakes, or to taste

½ teaspoon salt

4 cups mixed salad leaves

Juice of ½ lime

½ cup fresh coriander leaves

Heat oil in a large wok. Add the octopus, calamari, garlic, chilli and salt. Stir-fry for five minutes or until octopus and calamari are tender and cooked through. Allow to cool slightly before combining with the salad, lime juice and coriander. Toss well and serve.

Serves: 4
Total cooking time: 5 minutes preparation, 5 minutes cooking

Budget Meals

Haricot bean soup with tomatoes and parsley

Turkey omelette with zucchini and cherry tomatoes served with green salad

Risotto with basmati rice, spinach, and mixed herbs

Pork and eggplant stir-fry

Roast chicken served with steamed vegetables with butter and thyme

Baked ricotta with capsicum, sun-dried tomatoes and parsley

Mushroom noodle soup

Beef stir-fry with green beans and broccoli

Chicken breast stuffed with ricotta and semi sun-dried tomatoes served with chilli tomato sauce and rocket salad

Asparagus soup

Cayenne pepper and oregano chicken with mixed salad and grape tomatoes

Grilled fish fillets with mixed vegetables

Lamb cutlets with grilled zucchini and tomato salad

Tuna, bean and egg salad

Borlotti beans with sweet potato mash

Chicken kebabs with garlic aioli served with mustard-flavoured spinach

Tomato and fennel soup

Chicken and lemongrass stir-fry with mushrooms and green beans

Beef burgers with tomato sauce served with minted asparagus and squash

Chicken casserole

Scrambled eggs with tomato and mushroom

Shish-kebabs with tomato and basil salad

Lamb curry

Haricot bean soup with tomatoes and parsley

Carbohydrate

6 cups water

500g (16 oz) dried haricot beans, soaked in water
   overnight

1 onion, chopped

3 stalks of celery, thinly sliced

1 can diced tomatoes

1 tablespoon tomato paste

2 bay leaves

2 tablespoons finely chopped flat-leaf parsley leaves and
   stalks

Sea salt and freshly cracked black pepper to taste

In a large saucepan, bring water to the boil. Add beans, onion, celery, tomatoes, tomato paste and bay leaves; cover and simmer for 1½ hours or until beans are tender. Season and stir through parsley before serving.

Serves: 4
Total cooking time: 12 hours soaking, 5 minutes preparation, 1½ hours cooking

Turkey omelette with zucchini and cherry tomatoes served with green salad

Protein

Turkey omelette

1 tablespoon olive oil

½ onion, finely diced

1 zucchini, grated

6 cherry tomatoes, quartered

150g (5 oz) roast turkey breast, diced

6 eggs, lightly beaten

½ cup grated tasty cheese

Sea salt and freshly cracked black pepper to taste

Green salad

3 cups mixed green lettuce leaves

1 cucumber, halved, seeded and diced

½ green capsicum, seeded and thinly sliced

2 tablespoons olive oil

Sea salt and freshly cracked black pepper to taste

For the omelette, heat oil in a large frying pan, add onions and sauté until softened. Add zucchini, tomatoes and turkey and fry 2 minutes. Pour over egg, then season. Cook 10 minutes over low heat until set. Scatter over grated cheese then place under a hot grill until cheese has melted and top is lightly browned.

For the green salad, combine all ingredients together and toss well.

Serve omelette in wedges with salad to the side.

Serves: 4

Total cooking time: 5 minutes preparation, 25 minutes cooking

Risotto with basmati rice, spinach, and mixed herbs

Carbohydrate

7 cups hot vegetable stock

2 garlic cloves, crushed

2 leeks, thinly sliced

2 cups basmati rice

¼ cup white wine vinegar

2 tablespoons fresh flat-leaf parsley, chopped

1 tablespoon fresh oregano, chopped

1 tablespoon fresh thyme, chopped

12 semi sun-dried tomatoes, chopped

2 cups baby English spinach leaves

Sea salt and freshly cracked black pepper to taste

To a large frying pan add garlic and leeks with a little water and stir-fry until leeks begin to soften; add basmati rice and stir-fry for 3 minutes. Add half the vinegar and 1 cup of stock; cook over low heat until liquid is absorbed. Repeat adding the rest of the vinegar and 1 cup of stock at a time until the rice is soft and cooked through.

Stir through the mixed herbs, sun-dried tomatoes, baby spinach and seasoning; cook for a further 2 minutes, then serve.

Serves: 4

Total cooking time: 5 minutes preparation, 30 minutes cooking

Pork and eggplant stir-fry

Protein

Wom bok (used in this recipe) is a Chinese cabbage. It is very similar to ordinary cabbage but has the added benefit of cooking quicker.

2 eggplants, peeled and diced

1 tablespoon peanut oil

1 teaspoon sesame oil

1 teaspoon dried chilli flakes, or to taste

2 garlic cloves, crushed

4 spring onions, sliced

500g (16 oz) pork mince

3 cups wom bok, shredded

150g (5 oz) green snake beans, cut into 5 cm (2 inch) lengths

2 tablespoons fish sauce

1 cup fresh Thai basil leaves, chopped

Sea salt and freshly cracked black pepper to taste

In a saucepan of boiling water cook eggplant for 5 minutes; drain and gently squeeze of excess water.

Heat oils in a wok, then add chilli, garlic and spring onion; stir-fry for 2 minutes. Add pork and stir-fry 5 minutes or until browned. Add wom bok, green snake beans, eggplant and fish sauce, then stir-fry for 10 minutes or until vegetables are tender. Stir through basil leaves and seasoning, then serve.

Serves: 4

Total cooking time: 5 minutes preparation, 20 minutes cooking

Roast chicken served with steamed vegetables with butter and thyme

Protein

Roast chicken

1 medium chicken (about 1.5 kg or 13 lbs)

1 onion, halved

1 lemon, halved

4 tablespoons olive oil

Zest of 1 lemon

1 teaspoon dried oregano

Sea salt and freshly cracked black pepper to taste

Steamed vegetables

150g (5 oz) green beans, trimmed and halved

8 asparagus spears, trimmed and halved

1 zucchini cut into matchsticks

2 baby yellow squash, sliced

1 tablespoon butter, melted

½ teaspoon dried thyme

Sea salt and freshly cracked black pepper to taste

Stuff chicken cavity with the lemon and onion. Close cavity and tie legs together with kitchen string. Rub olive oil, lemon zest, oregano and seasoning into chicken skin. Place chicken on a baking tray and roast at 180°C (350°F) for 1½ hours or until browned and tender.

In a steamer, steam vegetables until tender. Toss through butter, thyme and seasoning.

Serve chicken with vegetables to the side.

Serves: 4

Total cooking time: 10 minutes preparation, 1½ hours cooking

Baked ricotta with capsicum, sun-dried tomatoes and parsley

Protein

1 kg (2 lbs) ricotta cheese

4 eggs, beaten lightly

1 red capsicum

1 yellow capsicum

10 sun-dried tomatoes

2 tablespoons fresh flat-leaf parsley leaves

Sea salt and freshly cracked black pepper to taste

Combine ricotta and eggs, then season. Pour the ricotta mixture into a non-stick cake tin. Bake at 180°C (350°F) for 35 minutes. Allow to cool before turning out onto a plate.

Grill capsicum until skin blackens and blisters. Place in a plastic bag to cool. Once cooled, peel, deseed and quarter.

Top baked ricotta with the capsicum, tomatoes and parsley; serve in wedges.

Serves: 4–6

Total cooking time: 10 minutes preparation, 35 minutes cooking

Mushroom noodle soup

Carbohydrate

This soup is similar to a Vietnamese-style hot and sour soup. Add extra chilli, or even sambal oelek, if you want an extra zing.

10 flat mushrooms, thinly sliced

1 Lebanese cucumber, halved, seeded and thinly sliced

2 spring onions, sliced

1 garlic clove, sliced

½ teaspoon chilli powder, or to taste

200g bean thread noodles

5 cups vegetable stock

3 tablespoons soy sauce

Juice of 1 lemon

Sea salt and freshly cracked black pepper to taste

Soak noodles in boiling hot water for 20 minutes then drain.
Combine all ingredients, including noodles in a large saucepan.
Bring soup to the boil then reduce heat and allow to simmer
10 minutes before serving.

Serves: 4
Total cooking time: 20 minutes preparation, 10 minutes cooking

Beef stir-fry with green beans and broccoli

Protein

200g (7 oz) greens beans, trimmed and cut into
    5 cm (2 inch) lengths

1 head of broccoli, cut into florettes

4 tablespoons olive oil

1 onion, sliced

1 stick celery, thinly sliced

500g (16 oz) beef, thinly sliced

1 tablespoon mixed dried herbs

Sea salt and freshly cracked black pepper to taste

Blanche beans and broccoli in boiling salted water for 1 minute; drain and set aside.

Heat oil in a large wok, add onion and celery and stir-fry until onion softens. Add beef and stir-fry for 4 minutes or until browned. Add beans, broccoli, herbs and seasoning and stir-fry a further 4 minutes before serving.

Serves: 4
Total cooking time: 5 minutes preparation, 10 minutes cooking

Chicken breast stuffed with ricotta and semi sun-dried tomatoes served with chilli tomato sauce and rocket salad

Protein

You can also cook this recipe on the barbecue by browning the stuffed chicken fillets all over then cooking with indirect heat in a covered barbecue for 15 minutes.

Chicken breast stuffed with ricotta

1 cup ricotta

½ cup finely grated Parmesan cheese

½ teaspoon chilli powder

50g (1½ oz) semi-dried tomatoes, finely chopped

4 chicken breasts fillets

2 tablespoons olive oil

Chilli tomato sauce

2 tablespoons vegetable oil

1 tablespoon red wine vinegar

2 tomato, seeded and chopped

Dash of chilli powder, or to taste

Dash of cayenne pepper, or to taste

½ teaspoon paprika

½ teaspoon salt

Rocket salad

4 cups rocket

2 tablespoons olive oil

Juice of ½ lemon

Combine ricotta, Parmesan cheese, chilli and tomatoes. Cut pockets into the side of the chicken breasts. Fill the pockets with the ricotta mixture and close with metal skewers. Heat oil in a frying pan and fry chicken over high heat for 2 minutes each side. Place chicken on a baking tray and bake for 15 minutes at 200°C (390°F).

For the chilli tomato sauce, process all ingredients in a blender until smooth. Place in a saucepan, bring to boil then allow to simmer for 10 minutes uncovered. Serve the sauce drizzled over the chicken.

For the rocket salad, combine all ingredients; toss well and serve to the side.

Serves: 4

Total cooking time: 10 minutes preparation, 20 minutes cooking

Asparagus soup

Protein

This soup is great in winter as an afternoon snack. Make up a big batch and freeze it in single serve containers.

1 tablespoon olive oil

2 tablespoons butter

1 onion, finely chopped

350g (12 oz) canned asparagus spears, drained

4 cups vegetable stock

¼ teaspoon ground coriander

1 tablespoon lemon juice

3 tablespoons sour cream

Sea salt and freshly cracked black pepper to taste

Heat oil and butter in a large saucepan, add onion and cook until softened. Add asparagus spears, chicken stock, coriander and lemon juice. Bring to boil then reduce heat and allow to simmer 10 minutes. In a food processor puree asparagus and stock mixture until smooth; return to saucepan. Stir through sour cream and seasoning, gently reheat, then serve.

Serves: 4
Total cooking time: 5 minutes preparation, 15 minutes cooking

Cayenne pepper and oregano chicken with mixed salad and grape tomatoes

Protein

Cayenne pepper and oregano chicken

½ cup olive oil

1 teaspoon salt

1 garlic clove, crushed

½ teaspoon cayenne pepper

1 tablespoon dried oregano

3 chicken breast fillets, quartered lengthways

4 cups of mixed salad leaves

12 grape tomatoes, halved

Dressing

Juice of ½ lemon

¼ cup olive oil, extra

Sea salt and freshly cracked black pepper to taste

Combine olive oil, salt, garlic, cayenne pepper and oregano; coat chicken with oil mixture. Cook for 3 minutes each side or until golden brown and cooked through. Divide salad leaves and tomatoes between four plates; top salad with chicken pieces. For the dressing, combine lemon and olive oil; mix well then drizzle over the chicken and salad, then season.

Serves: 4
Total cooking time: 5 minutes preparation, 6 minutes cooking

Grilled fish fillets with mixed vegetables

Protein

Grilled fish fillets

4 fish fillets

2 tablespoons olive oil

Sea salt and freshly cracked black pepper to taste

Mixed vegetables

2 tablespoons olive oil

1 onion, finely chopped

1 red capsicum, seeded and chopped

3 tomatoes, chopped

2 baby yellow squash, chopped

1 zucchini, chopped

2 tablespoons white wine vinegar

½ cup fresh flat-leaf parsley, chopped

Sea salt and freshly cracked black pepper to taste

2 tablespoons fresh flat-leaf parsley, chopped, extra to garnish

Heat oil in a large frying pan. Season fish fillets then fry for 2–3 minutes each side or until just cooked.

For the mixed vegetables, heat oil in a large saucepan, add onion and cook until softened. Add all other ingredients and cook for 15 minutes, uncovered, or until fluid is reduced.

Serve vegetables mixture onto 4 plates and top with the fish fillets. Serve garnished with extra parsley.

Serves: 4

Total cooking time: 5 minutes preparation, 20 minutes cooking

Lamb cutlets with grilled zucchini and tomato salad

Protein

Lamb cutlets

12 lamb cutlets

2 tablespoons olive oil

1 clove of garlic, crushed

1 tablespoon dried oregano

½ teaspoon salt

½ teaspoon pepper

Grilled zucchini and tomato salad

2 tablespoons olive oil

2 zucchini, sliced 1 cm (½ inch) thick lengthways

4 Roma tomatoes, halved

Sea salt and freshly cracked black pepper to taste

Combine olive oil, garlic, oregano, salt and pepper. Baste lamb cutlets with the oil and herb mixture, then grill on the barbecue for 3 minutes each side.

For the grilled zucchini and tomato salad, brush zucchini and tomatoes with olive oil, then barbecue 3 minutes each side or until tender and cooked through, then season. Serve lamb with zucchini and tomatoes to the side.

Serves: 4
Total cooking time: 5 minutes preparation, 10 minutes cooking

Tuna, bean and egg salad

Protein

This recipe can be used as a light lunch in summer, or served as part of a barbecue buffet. I have used plain vinegar and mixed herbs in this recipe to keep the cost down, however, if you would like to spice it up, then use white wine vinegar, 2 table-spoons of freshly chopped parsley and 1 tablespoon of freshly chopped mint.

425g (15 oz) tuna in oil

200g (7 oz) green beans, cut into 5 cm (2 inch) lengths

4 hard boiled eggs, halved

8 cups of mixed salad leaves

1 cucumber, sliced

150g (5 oz) grape tomatoes, halved

1 tablespoon mixed dried herbs

2 tablespoons vinegar

Sea salt and freshly cracked black pepper to taste

Cook beans in boiling salted water until just tender, then drain. Combine beans and all other ingredients together, including the tuna oil, then toss well and serve.

Serves: 4

Total cooking time: 10 minutes preparation

Borlotti beans with sweet potato mash

Carbohydrate

Borlotti beans

400g (14 oz) canned borlotti beans, drained

400g (14 oz) canned diced tomatoes

1 tablespoon tomato paste

2 tablespoons vinegar

1 tablespoon mixed dried herbs

Sea salt and freshly cracked black pepper to taste

Sweet potato mash

2 large sweet potato, peeled and cut into chunks

1 garlic clove, crushed

1 teaspoon ground cumin

1 tablespoon fresh flat-leaf parsley leaves

Sea salt and freshly cracked black pepper to taste

Place beans, tomatoes, tomato paste, vinegar, herbs and seasoning in a large saucepan. Bring to the boil then allow to simmer uncovered for 10 minutes, stirring frequently.

For the sweet potato mash, cook the potatoes in boiling salted water until very soft. Drain then mash potatoes. Add garlic, cumin, parsley and seasoning to mashed potatoes, mix well.

Serve potato with borlotti beans poured over.

Serves: 4

Total cooking time: 5 minutes preparation, 20 minutes cooking

Chicken kebabs with garlic aioli served with mustard-flavoured spinach

Protein

Mustard oil should be available in your local delicatessen. It adds a wonderful flavour to the spinach. If you can not find mustard oil, or you find it is too expensive, then substitute with olive oil, vegetable oil or even butter.

Chicken kebabs
500g (16 oz) diced chicken
2 tablespoons olive oil
Sea salt and freshly cracked black pepper to taste

Garlic aioli
2 egg yolks
2 garlic cloves, crushed
Juice of ½ lemon
½ cup olive oil
Sea salt and freshly cracked black pepper to taste

Mustard-flavoured spinach
2 tablespoons mustard oil
¼ teaspoon garam masala
1 teaspoon mustard seeds
500g (16 oz) baby English spinach leaves
2 spring onions, sliced
1 tablespoon mustard oil, extra
Sea salt and freshly cracked black pepper to taste

Thread diced chicken onto skewers, baste with oil and season. Cook chicken skewers on a heated oiled barbecue for 5 minutes each side or until golden brown and cooked through.

For the garlic aioli, combine egg yolks, garlic and lemon juice. Gradually add the olive oil, whisking continuously, until aioli thickens, then season. Briefly pulse in a blender until smooth.

For the mustard-flavoured spinach, heat mustard oil in a large frying pan, add garam masala and mustard seed and stir-fry 1 minute covered, or until mustard seeds have all popped. Add spring onions and spinach and cook 8 minutes or until spinach has wilted. Stir through extra mustard oil and seasoning.

Serve chicken kebabs on top of the spinach and drizzle over the aioli.

Serve: 4
Makes: 8 skewers
Total cooking time: 5 minutes preparation, 12 minutes cooking

Tomato and fennel soup

Protein

Fennel is an aniseed-smelling vegetable that is actually similar in character to celery in terms of texture and cooking. You should cut off the bottom of the bulb and trim any tough stalks from the top of the bulb. If there are any green fronds on the top of the bulb then chop these up and add them to the soup.

2 tablespoons olive oil

1 onion, finely chopped

1 stick of celery, finely sliced

½ fennel bulb, finely sliced

800g (28 oz) canned diced tomatoes

3 cups chicken stock

1 tablespoon tomato paste

1 tablespoon mixed dried herbs

Sea salt and freshly cracked black pepper to taste

Heat oil in a large saucepan, add onion, celery and fennel and cook until onion softens. Add all other ingredients, bring to the boil then allow to simmer covered for 10 minutes.

Serves: 4

Total cooking time: 5 minutes preparation, 15 minutes cooking

Chicken and lemongrass stir-fry with mushrooms and green beans

Protein

Lemongrass is an Asian herb. It should be peeled of the tough outer leaves and trimmed so that only the white part closer to the base is used.

3 tablespoons peanut oil

500g (16 oz) diced chicken

1 garlic clove, crushed

1 birds-eye chilli, finely chopped

1 stick of fresh lemongrass, finely sliced

10 button mushrooms, halved

200g (7 oz) green snake beans, cut in 5 cm (2 inch) lengths

2 tablespoons fish sauce

2 spring onions, sliced

Sea salt and freshly cracked black pepper to taste

Heat oil in a large wok, then add chicken, garlic, chilli and lemongrass. Stir-fry until chicken is lightly browned. Add the mushrooms and green snake beans and stir-fry for 5 minutes. Add fish sauce, spring onions and seasoning, then serve.

Serves: 4

Total cooking time: 5 minutes preparation, 12 minutes cooking

Beef burgers with tomato sauce served with minted asparagus and squash

Protein

Beef burgers

500g (16 oz) beef mince

1 garlic clove, crushed

1 egg white, lightly beaten

2 teaspoons mixed dried herbs

½ teaspoon sea salt

¼ teaspoon freshly ground black pepper

Tomato sauce

1 tablespoon oil

½ onion, finely chopped

1 bay leaf

2 cloves

400g (14 oz) canned diced tomatoes

1 tablespoon tomato paste

1 tablespoon white wine vinegar

Sea salt and freshly cracked black pepper to taste

Minted asparagus and squash

2 tablespoons olive oil

1 red onion, sliced

1 bunch thin asparagus, trimmed and quartered

4 yellow squash, sliced

1 tablespoon finely chopped mint

Juice and zest of ½ lemon

Sea salt and coarsely ground black pepper

For the burgers, combine beef, garlic, egg white, mixed herbs and seasoning. Form meat mixture into 20 burgers. Cook burgers in a frying pan or on a barbecue plate for 3 minutes each side or until browned and cooked through.

For the tomato sauce, heat oil in a frying pan, add onions and cook until softened. Add bay leaf, cloves, tomatoes, tomato paste and vinegar. Bring to the boil then reduce heat and allow to simmer for 10 minutes, uncovered. Remove bay leaf and cloves, then process sauce in a blender until smooth. Season sauce to taste.

For the minted asparagus and squash, heat oil in a wok, add onion and cook until softened. Add asparagus and squash and stir-fry 3 minutes, add lemon juice and zest, and seasoning to taste; continue to stir-fry a further 2 minutes, or until vegetables have just started to soften. Remove from heat and stir through mint.

Serve burgers with tomato sauce drizzled over them and asparagus and mint to the side.

Serves: 4
Total cooking time: 5 minutes preparation, 15 minutes cooking

Chicken casserole

Protein

500g (16 oz) diced chicken breast

1 tablespoon mixed dried herbs

2 cloves garlic, finely chopped

½ teaspoon sea salt

¼ teaspoon freshly ground black pepper

4 tablespoons olive oil

2 brown onions, finely chopped

2 zucchini, sliced

6 tablespoons olive oil

400g (14 oz) canned diced tomatoes

2 tablespoons chopped fresh flat-leaf parsley

Sea salt and freshly cracked black pepper to taste

Combine chicken, herbs, garlic and seasoning, mix well. Heat 2 tablespoons of the oil in a large wok; add chicken and stir-fry 6 minutes or until chicken is cooked through and golden brown; set chicken aside. Add remaining oil to the wok; add onion and zucchini to the pan and stir-fry 5 minutes. Add tomatoes and chicken, cover and simmer 10 minutes. Stir through parsley, extra seasoning and serve.

Serves: 4
Total cooking time: 5 minutes preparation, 20 minutes cooking

Scrambled eggs with tomato and mushroom

Protein

Very simple but very tasty. This recipe is good for when there is hardly anything left in the cupboard, you are too tired to shop, and you are hungry right now – don't get take-away, cook this, it is easy.

1 tablespoon oil

2 tablespoons butter

1 onion, sliced

1 garlic clove, crushed

10 button mushrooms, sliced

2 tomatoes, cut into wedges

1 teaspoon dried oregano

8 eggs, lightly beaten

2 tablespoons cream

¼ teaspoon salt

Dash of pepper

Heat oil and butter in a large frying pan, add the onion and garlic, then cook until onions soften. Add the mushrooms and stir-fry for 5 minutes. Add the tomato and herbs and cook a further 2 minutes.

Combine eggs, cream and seasoning; pour mixture over the tomato and mushrooms. Cook over low heat for 3 minutes, stirring frequently until cooked. Serve garnished with fresh flat-leaf parsley.

Serves: 4
Total cooking time: 5 minutes preparation, 12 minutes cooking

Shish-kebabs with tomato and baby spinach leaf salad

Protein

Shish-kebabs

500g (16 oz) mince beef

½ teaspoon chilli powder

1 tablespoon ground cumin

1 teaspoon ground coriander

1 teaspoon salt

½ teaspoon ground black pepper

1 egg white, lightly beaten

Tomato and baby spinch leaf salad

100g (3½ oz) baby English spinach leaves

2 tomatoes cut into 8 wedges each

2 tablespoons olive oil

½ tablespoon white wine vinegar

Sea salt and freshly cracked black pepper to taste

Combine beef, chilli, cumin, coriander, salt, pepper and egg white. Mix well then squeeze meat around the ends of 12 skewers. Cook shish-kebabs in a frying pan or on a barbecue plate for 5 minutes each side or until browned and cooked through.

For the salad, arrange spinach leaves onto 4 plates, top with tomato wedges, drizzle over the olive oil and vinegar and season.

Serve shish-kebabs with salad to the side.

Serves: 4

Total cooking time: 5 minutes preparation, 6 minutes cooking

Lamb curry
Protein

This recipe gets a gold star rating from John. Use less garlic and curry if you have children to feed; use more if you have adults with steel palates to feed. You can even add a little chilli if you like.

1 tablespoon oil

2 onions, sliced

2 garlic cloves, crushed

600g (20 oz) diced lamb

½ teaspoon pepper

2 teaspoons turmeric

2 teaspoons ground coriander

1 tablespoon mild curry powder

2 zucchini, sliced

2 baby yellow squash, sliced

150g (5 oz) green snake beans, trimmed and cut into
    5 cm (2 inch) lengths

Juice of ½ lime

2 tablespoons sour cream

1 teaspoon salt

Heat oil in a large saucepan, add onions and garlic and cook until onion softens. Add lamb, pepper, turmeric, coriander and curry powder and stir-fry 5 minutes over high heat or until meat is browned all over. Add the zucchini, squash and beans and stir-fry a further 10 minutes. Add lime juice, cream and salt; gently heat then serve.

Serves: 4
Total cooking time: 5 minutes preparation, 15 minutes cooking

Fast barbecue ideas

Spicy barbecued chicken thighs with lemon and oregano dressing

*Barbecued prawns with basil, chilli and kaffir lime leaves
served with an Asian salad*

*Beef and haloumi kebabs with horseradish, drizzled with caper
and oregano butter*

*Steaks rubbed with roasted capsicum, sun-dried tomato and basil
served with caper and rocket salad*

Lamb, eggplant and capsicum skewers with sumac and thyme

*Crab and prawn cakes with chilli and ginger served with chilli
and lime dressing*

*Grilled mixed vegetables and haloumi cheese with cumin and
lemon thyme dressing*

Sichuan lamb skewers served with stir-fried ginger wom bok

Beef burgers drizzled with avocado dressing

Vietnamese fish skewers served with mixed green salad

Barbecued vegetables drizzled with green chilli and tomato sauce

Skewered prawns served with Greek salad

Turkish chicken kebabs served with spinach with sumac and mint

Spicy barbecued chicken thighs with lemon and oregano dressing

Protein

Spicy chicken thighs

2 teaspoons cracked black pepper

1 tablespoon paprika

1 teaspoon chilli powder

1 teaspoon salt

1 teaspoon cayenne pepper

1 teaspoon ground coriander

12 chicken thigh fillets, halved

Lemon and oregano dressing

1 teaspoon dried oregano leaves

1 garlic clove, crushed

Juice of 1 lemon

2 tablespoons white wine vinegar

¼ cup olive oil

Sea salt and freshly cracked black pepper to taste

Combine pepper, paprika, chilli powder, salt, cayenne pepper and coriander. Rub mixture into the chicken thigh fillets. Grill on the barbecue for 10 minutes or until browned and cooked through. Turn once during cooking.

Combine oregano, garlic, lemon juice, vinegar, olive oil and seasoning, whisk together well.

Serve chicken thighs with lemon and oregano vinaigrette drizzled over.

Serves: 6
Total cooking time: 10 minutes preparation, 10 minutes cooking

Barbecued prawns with basil, chilli and kaffir lime leaves served with an Asian salad

Protein

Barbecued prawns

4 kaffir lime leaves, finely sliced

¼ cup fresh Thai basil leaves, chopped

Juice and rind of 2 limes

¼ cup peanut oil

1 fresh birds-eye chilli, seeded and chopped

1 garlic clove, crushed

2 teaspoons fish sauce

1 kg (2 lbs) large prawns, peeled, deveined, tails left intact

Asian salad

4 cups mixed salad leaves

½ Lebanese cucumber, sliced

¼ cup Thai basil leaves, shredded

¼ cup Vietnamese mint leaves, shredded

½ red capsicum, seeded and sliced

1 tablespoon lime juice

2 tablespoons peanut oil

Combine all barbecued prawns ingredients together. Refrigerate and allow to marinate for 20 minutes. Cook prawns on the barbecue for 2 minutes each side or until cooked through.

For the Asian salad combine all ingredients and toss well.

Serve prawns with salad to the side.

Serves: 4

Total cooking time: 10 minutes preparation, 5 minutes cooking

Beef and haloumi kebabs with horseradish, drizzled with caper and oregano butter

Protein

Beef and haloumi kebabs

8 bamboo skewers, soaked in water for 1 hour

1 kg (2 lbs) rump steak, cubed

2 tablespoons olive oil

1 tablespoon grated lemon rind

2 tablespoons lemon juice

1 tablespoon fresh horseradish, grated

Sea salt and freshly cracked pepper to taste

400g (14 oz) haloumi cheese, cubed

Caper butter

2 tablespoons drained capers, chopped finely

1 teaspoon dried oregano

100g (3½ oz) butter, melted

Dash of freshly cracked pepper

Combine beef, oil, lemon juice and rind, horseradish and seasoning. Refrigerate for 3 hours.

Thread beef and cheese onto the skewers and cook on heated barbecue until browned and meat is cooked through.

For the caper butter, melt butter in a small saucepan, add capers and stir over medium heat for 3 minutes.

Serve skewers onto plates with caper butter poured over.

Serves: 4

Total cooking time: 3 hours marinating, 10 minutes preparation

Steaks rubbed with roasted capsicum, sun-dried tomato and basil served with caper and rocket salad

Protein

Steaks

4 beef steaks

2 large red capsicums

½ cup sun-dried tomatoes in oil, drained

1 tablespoon olive oil

2 tablespoons finely chopped fresh basil leaves

Sea salt and freshly cracked black pepper to taste

Caper and rocket salad

3 cups of rocket leaves

1 tablespoon olive oil

1 tablespoon lemon juice

2 teaspoons baby salted capers

Sea salt and freshly cracked black pepper to taste

Roast capsicum for 20 minutes at 220°C (420°F) or until skin blackens and blisters. Allow to cool in a plastic bag before removing skin and seeds. Place capsicum, tomatoes, olive oil and basil in a blender and process until smooth; season to taste.

Baste the steaks with the capsicum pesto and grill on a barbecue until cooked as desired.

For the caper and rocket salad, combine all ingredients together and toss well.

Serve steaks with caper and rocket salad to the side.

Serves: 4

Total cooking time: 5 minutes preparation, 30 minutes cooking

Lamb, eggplant and capsicum skewers with sumac and thyme

Protein

3 red capsicums, seeded and cut into 5 cm (2 inch) pieces

4 baby eggplants, sliced 2 cm thick

300g (9½ oz) diced lamb

12 skewers

⅓ cup olive oil

2 garlic cloves, crushed

1 teaspoon sumac

1 teaspoon fresh thyme leaves, finely chopped

Alternately thread capsicum, eggplant and lamb onto skewers. Combine olive oil, garlic, sumac, thyme, lemon juice and zest. Baste skewers with the oil marinade. Cook skewers on the barbecue for 4 minutes each side or until cooked through, baste frequently with any remaining marinade.

Serves: 4
Total cooking time: 10 minutes preparation, 8 minutes cooking

Crab and prawn cakes with chilli and ginger served with chilli and lime dressing

Protein

Crab and prawn cakes

400g (14 oz) prawn meat

200g (7 oz) shredded crab meat

½ to 1 birds-eye chilli (as per taste), seeded and finely
chopped

1 teaspoon fresh ginger, grated

¼ teaspoon of salt

1 egg white, lightly beaten

Chilli and lime dressing

½ long red chilli, finely chopped

½ garlic clove, crushed

Juice of 1 lime

2 teaspoons fish sauce

1 tablespoon apple cider vinegar

*Process prawn meat, crab meat, chilli, ginger, salt and egg in a
blender. Form mixture into approximately 16 patties. Cook patties
on an oiled barbecue pate for 2–3 minutes each side.*

*For the chilli and lime dressing, combine all ingredients together in
a jar and shake well.*

Serve dressing with the crab and prawn cakes.

Makes: 16 patties

Total cooking time: 10 minutes preparation, 5 minutes cooking

Grilled mixed vegetables and haloumi cheese with cumin and lemon thyme dressing

Protein

Grilled mixed vegetables and haloumi cheese

2 yellow zucchinis, sliced thickly lengthways

2 green zucchinis, sliced thickly lengthways

2 red capsicums, seeded and sliced thickly lengthways

2 yellow capsicums, seeded and sliced thickly lengthways

4 baby eggplants, halved lengthways

3 Roma tomatoes, halved lengthways

4 spring onions, trimmed

200g (7 oz) haloumi cheese, sliced 1 cm (½ inch) thick

Cumin and lemon thyme dressing

4 tablespoons olive oil

1 teaspoon caraway seeds

Juice and rind of ½ lemon

1 garlic clove, crushed

2 teaspoons ground cumin

1 tablespoon fresh oregano leaves, chopped

1 tablespoon fresh lemon thyme, finely chopped

2 tablespoons baby salted capers

Sea salt and freshly ground black pepper to taste

Grill all vegetables and haloumi cheese on the barbecue until browned and tender. Combine oil, caraway seeds, lemon rind, garlic, cumin, oregano, thyme and capers; drizzle over grilled vegetables and cheese, season and toss well to combine. Serve hot or cold.

Serves: 6
Total cooking time: 10 minutes preparation, 15 minutes cooking

Sichuan lamb skewers served with stir-fried ginger wom bok

Protein

Sichuan lamb skewers

1 tablespoon cumin, ground

1 teaspoon Sichuan peppercorns, ground

1 teaspoon chilli powder, or to taste

Pinch of white pepper

1 teaspoon salt

½ cup vegetable oil

2 teaspoons sesame oil

1 kg (2 lbs) diced lamb

12 bamboo skewers, soaked in water for 30 minutes

Ginger wom bok

2 tablespoons peanut oil

4 cups shredded wom bok

1 teaspoon freshly grated ginger

¼ cup apple cider vinegar

Sea salt and freshly cracked black pepper to taste

For the Sichuan lamb skewers, combine all ingredients. Cover and refrigerate for 2–3 hours. After marinating, thread lamb onto skewers, then barbecue for 3 minutes each side or until lamb is tender.

For the ginger wom bok, heat oil in a large wok, add the wom bok and ginger and stir-fry for 3 minutes. Add the vinegar and half a cup of water. Cover the wok, reduce heat and allow to simmer for 5 minutes, stir occasionally.

Serve lamb skewers with the ginger wom bok to the side.

Makes: 10 kebabs
Total cooking time: 5 minutes preparation, 3 hours marinating,
10 minutes cooking

Beef burgers drizzled with avocado dressing

Protein

Beef burgers

1 garlic clove, crushed

½ onion, minced

¼ cup sun-dried tomatoes, chopped

½ teaspoon sea salt

¼ teaspoon freshly ground black pepper

500g (16 oz) mince beef

1 egg whites, lightly beaten

Avocado dressing

2 egg yolks, lightly beaten

Juice of ½ lemon

½ cup olive oil

½ avocado, mashed

Sea salt and freshly ground black pepper to taste

In a food processor combine garlic, onion, sun-dried tomatoes, seasoning, mince and egg whites. Form mixture into 12 patties. Cook on the barbecue for 5 minutes each side or until brown and cooked through.

For the avocado dressing, combine yolks and lemon juice, then gradually add olive oil while whisking. In a food processor combine the aioli with the avocado and blend well, season.

Drizzle avocado dressing over the burgers and serve with mixed salad leaves drizzled with a little extra olive oil.

Serves: 4

Total cooking time: 10 minutes preparation, 10 minutes cooking

Vietnamese fish skewers served with mixed green salad

Protein

Fish skewers

1 kg (2 lbs) firm white fish fillets, cut into 2 cm (1 inch)
   pieces

1 tablespoon fresh Vietnamese mint leaves, chopped

1 tablespoon fresh coriander leaves, chopped

1 tablespoon fresh flat-leaf parsley leaves, chopped

1 fresh red birds-eye chilli, finely chopped

Juice of 1 lime

1 tablespoon peanut oil

12 skewers

Sea salt and freshly cracked black pepper to taste

Mixed green salad

3 cups mixed Asian salad leaves

1 Lebanese cucumber, sliced

1 fresh long red chilli, seeded and chopped

1 cup bamboo shoots

½ red capsicum, seeded and sliced

½ green capsicum, seeded and sliced

1 tablespoon vegetable oil

Juice of ½ lime

For the fish skewers, combine all ingredients, toss well to coat fish in the marinade. Thread fish pieces onto the skewers, then barbecue for 2 minutes each side or until browned and cooked through.

For the salad, combine all ingredients together and toss well.

Serve fish skewers onto plates and lightly season. Serve salad to the side.

Serves: 4
Total Cooking Time: 10 minutes preparation, 4 minutes cooking

Barbecued vegetables drizzled with green chilli and tomato sauce

Protein

Barbecued vegetables

¼ cup olive oil

1 garlic clove, crushed

1 tablespoon fresh thyme leaves, chopped

1 tablespoon fresh rosemary, chopped

1 tablespoon fresh flat-leaf parsley leaves, chopped

1 red capsicum, seeded and quartered

1 yellow capsicum, seeded and quartered

3 zucchinis, halved then sliced 1 cm (½ inch) thick
   lengthways

2 baby yellow squash, sliced 1 cm (½ inch) thick

4 Roma tomatoes, halved

1 eggplant, sliced 1 cm (½ inch) thick

Sea salt and freshly cracked black pepper to taste

Green chilli and tomato sauce

2 tablespoons peanut oil

1 tablespoon sesame oil

1 garlic clove, crushed

1 onion, finely chopped

1 celery stick, finely chopped

1 long green chilli, seeded and chopped

400g (14 oz) canned diced tomatoes

Juice of ½ lemon

Sea salt and freshly cracked black pepper to taste

For the barbecued vegetables combine olive oil, garlic, thyme, rosemary, parsley and the vegetables. Toss well then refrigerate for 1 hour.

Barbecue vegetables 5–8 minutes, or until tender and cooked through; turn once during cooking.

For the green chilli and tomato sauce, heat oils in a small saucepan; add the garlic and onion, and cook until onion softens. Add the celery, chilli, tomatoes and lemon juice. Bring to the boil, then reduce heat and allow to simmer for 10 minutes or until the sauce thickens. Season to taste. Once cooked, arrange vegetables onto plates and season. Serve with the green chilli and tomato sauce drizzled over vegetables.

Serves: 4
Total cooking time: 15 minutes preparation, 1 hour marinating,
10 minutes cooking

Skewered prawns served with Greek salad

Protein

Skewered prawns

16 large uncooked prawns, peeled and deveined

1 garlic clove, crushed

1 tablespoon fresh oregano, chopped

1 tablespoon fresh flat-leaf parsley leaves, chopped

Juice of 1 lemon

1 tablespoon olive oil

Greek salad

200g (7 oz) feta cheese

1 red onion, thinly sliced

1 continental cucumber, sliced

5 tomatoes, cut into wedges

2 teaspoons fresh oregano, chopped

2 tablespoons fresh flat-leaf parsley leaves, chopped

1 garlic clove, crushed

Juice of 1 lemon

2 tablespoons olive oil

Sea salt and freshly cracked black pepper to taste

Thread each prawn lengthways onto a skewer. Combine garlic, oregano, parsley, lemon juice and olive oil. Baste the prawn skewers with the dressing. Cook the prawns on the barbecue for 3–4 minutes, turn once during cooking and baste frequently with the dressing.

For the Greek salad combine all ingredients together, toss well.

Serve prawns onto 4 plates with salad to the side.

Serves: 4

Total cooking time: 10 minutes preparation, 5 minutes cooking

Turkish chicken kebabs served with spinach with sumac and mint

Protein

Turkish chicken kebabs

750g (24 oz) chicken mince

1 red onion, minced

2 garlic cloves, crushed

½ teaspoon chilli flakes, or to taste

½ teaspoon cinnamon

1 teaspoon ground allspice

2 teaspoons ground cumin

2 teaspoons dried thyme

½ teaspoon salt

1 egg white, lightly beaten

Spinach with sumac and mint

1 tablespoon vegetable oil

300g (9½ oz) baby spinach leaves

½ teaspoon sumac

¼ cup fresh mint leaves, chopped

Sea salt and freshly cracked black pepper to taste

For the Turkish chicken kebabs, combine all ingredients together. Squeeze mixture onto 16 metal skewers. Cook kebabs on a barbecue plate for 3 minutes each side or until browned and cooked through.

For the spinach with sumac and mint, heat oil in a frying pan, add the spinach leaves and sumac and cook for 1–2 minutes until spinach has just wilted. Stir through mint and seasoning.

Serve kebabs with spinach to the side.

Serves: 4

Total cooking time: 5 minutes preparation, 10 minutes cooking

Workday lunches

Grilled mussel omelette with parsley

Beef stir-fry with chilli, green beans and walnuts

Sashimi salmon salad with wasabi and lime dressing

Basil and sun-dried tomato tartlets

Chicken wrapped in vine leaves with thyme and fennel

Performax sandwiches with oregano and mustard vinaigrette

Egg roll-ups

Spinach roulade with mushroom and cheese filling

Tofu balls with salad

Radicchio and feta rolls

Fish fillets wrapped in vine leaves with saffron, leeks and parsley

*Cajun spiced basmati rice salad with tomatoes, red kidney beans
and fresh herbs*

Feta, sun-dried tomato and prosciutto rolls with rocket salad

Salad with sumac

Omelette with salmon, sour cream and fresh herbs

Roasted Lebanese eggplant with capsicum, feta and rocket

*Radicchio and rocket salad with cherry tomatoes, prosciutto
and Parmesan cheese*

Burghul and chickpea salad with mandarins

Lamb and vegetable kebabs

Smoked salmon, caper, tarragon and dill muffins

Risotto with artichoke and fennel

Asian prawn salad with chilli and lime dressing

Baked ricotta tarts with roast tomatoes and basil

Grilled mussel omelette with parsley

Protein

1 kg (2 lbs) mussels

8 eggs, lightly beaten

2 tablespoons fresh flat-leaf parsley leaves, chopped

Sea salt and freshly cracked black pepper to taste

2 tablespoons olive oil

To a large frying pan add mussels and 2 tablespoons of water; cover and fry 3 minutes until shells open. Remove from heat and discard any unopened shells. Remove mussels from shells and chop roughly. Combine mussel meat with eggs, parsley and seasoning. In a frying pan heat olive oil, pour in egg and mussel mixture and cook 4–5 minutes before placing under a hot grill until lightly browned.

Keep refrigerated and re-heat for lunch.

Serves: 4
Total cooking time: 5 minutes preparation, 15 minutes cooking

Beef stir-fry with chilli, green beans and walnuts

Protein

2 tablespoons peanut oil

2 teaspoons sesame oil

1 onion, sliced

500g (16 oz) beef, thinly sliced

1 garlic clove, crushed

1 teaspoon grated fresh ginger

200g (7 oz) green snake beans, trimmed and cut into
   5 cm (2 inch) lengths

1 head of broccoli, cut into florets

¼ cup walnut pieces

2 tablespoons fish sauce

1 teaspoon dried chilli flakes

Heat oil in a large wok, add the onion and garlic and cook until onion softens. Remove onion and set aside. Place beef and ginger in the wok and stir-fry until beef is well browned.

In boiling salted water, blanch beans and broccoli for 1 minute. Drain and rinse under cold water. Add beans, broccoli, onion, walnut, fish sauce and chilli to the wok. Stir-fry for 2 minutes over high heat, then serve.

Keep refrigerated and re-heat for a workday lunch.

Serves: 4
Total cooking time: 5 minutes preparation, 20 minutes cooking

Sashimi salmon salad with wasabi and lime dressing

Protein

1 teaspoon sesame oil

1 tablespoon lime juice

½ to 1 teaspoon wasabi paste, or as per taste

1 tablespoon water

400g (14 oz) sashimi-grade salmon, sliced

2 spring onions, finely sliced

1 lime, peeled and finely chopped

¼ cup fresh coriander leaves

4 cups mixed salad leaves of choice

Combine sesame oil, lime juice, wasabi paste and water; set dressing aside. Combine salmon, onions, lime, coriander and salad leaves; pour over dressing; toss to combine then serve onto 4 plates. Keep refrigerated until ready to eat for a workday lunch.

Serves: 4
Total cooking time: 10 minutes preparation

Basil and sun-dried tomato tartlets

Protein

100g (3½ oz) mascarpone

500g (16 oz) ricotta

4 eggs

¼ teaspoon sea salt

½ cup fresh basil leaves, chopped

¼ cup semi-sundried tomatoes, finely diced

90g (3 oz) Parmesan cheese, freshly grated

Combine all ingredients together in a food processor until well blended. Pour mixture into greased muffin tins. Bake at 180°C (350°F) for 35 minutes or until set.

Makes: 10 tartlets
Total cooking time: 10 minutes preparation, 35 minutes cooking

Chicken wrapped in vine leaves with thyme and fennel

Protein

1 baby fennel, trimmed and finely chopped

1 garlic clove, crushed

½ red capsicum, seeded and finely chopped

½ green capsicum, seeded and finely chopped

8 cherry tomatoes, halved

1 teaspoon fresh thyme leaves,

Juice of ½ lemon

2 tablespoons white wine vinegar

2 tablespoons olive oil

Sea salt and freshly cracked black pepper to taste

12 vine leaves

2 chicken breasts fillets, halved lengthways

Combine fennel, garlic, capsicum, tomato, thyme, lemon juice, vinegar, olive oil and seasoning. Place 3 vine leaves each on 4 large squares of foil. Place chicken fillets on top of the vine leaves; spoon over fennel and thyme mixture and wrap vine leaves around to form a parcel. Fold up the foil edges to enclose the chicken wraps, sealing tightly. Cook the chicken for 25 minutes at 200°C (350°F).

Great for lunches; keep refrigerated and reheat when you are ready to eat.

Serves: 4

Total cooking time: 10 minutes preparation, 25 minutes cooking

Performax sandwiches with oregano and mustard vinaigrette

Carbohydrate

Yes, you can still eat a sandwich and here's a simple sandwich solution. If you use another brand of bread it must have a recorded GI lower than 50 and contain minimal fats.

Performax sandwich

Performax bread (Country Life Bakeries) or equivalent

Tomato, sliced

Cucumber, sliced

Alfalfa

Rocket leaves or other salad leaves of choice

Oregano and mustard vinaigrette

1 tablespoon white wine vinegar

1 tablespoon water

1 teaspoon lemon juice

½ teaspoon dried oregano

¼ teaspoon mustard powder

Sea salt and freshly cracked black pepper to taste

Fill sandwiches with tomato, cucumber, alfalfa and rocket. For the dressing, combine all ingredients in a jar, shake well then drizzle over sandwich filling.

Total cooking time: 5 minutes preparation

Egg roll-ups

Protein

6 eggs, lightly beaten

¼ teaspoon salt

¼ teaspoon pepper

2 tablespoons olive oil

2 tomatoes, diced

1 avocado, diced

1 cup rocket

Juice of ½ lemon

2 tablespoons olive oil

Combine eggs and seasoning. Heat oil in a large frying pan, cook a quarter of the egg mixture to form a thin crepe, repeat with the remaining egg mixture. Fill crepes with tomato, avocado and rocket, drizzle over lemon juice and olive oil; season then roll up the crepe.

Makes: 4 roll-ups
Serves: 4
Total cooking time: 5 minutes preparation, 10 minutes cooking

Spinach roulade with mushroom and cheese filling

Protein

Spinach roulade

2 tablespoons olive oil

250g (8 oz) frozen spinach, thawed and squeezed of
    excess fluid

Sea salt and freshly cracked black pepper to taste

4 egg yolks, lightly beaten

4 egg whites, stiffly beaten

½ cup Parmesan cheese, freshly grated

Mushroom and cheese filling

2 tablespoons butter

10 button mushrooms, thinly sliced

3 tablespoons cream

1 tablespoon of butter

½ cup grated Parmesan cheese

½ cup grated tasty cheese

2 egg yolks

¼ teaspoon nutmeg

¼ cup fresh flat-leaf parsley, chopped

Sea salt and freshly cracked black pepper to taste

*Heat oil in a large frying pan, then add the spinach and toss over
a high heat for about 1 minute. Remove from heat add seasoning
and egg yolks, then fold through egg whites. Place in a large
square greased baking tin lined with greased baking paper, top
with Parmesan cheese and bake for 15 minutes at 200°C
(390°F).*

For the mushroom and cheese filling, heat butter in saucepan, add mushrooms and fry 5 minutes.

In a saucepan melt extra butter, then add cream and cheeses; warm over very low heat until the cheese has melted. Remove from heat and allow to cool slightly, then add 2 egg yolks and whisk together well. Return sauce to the heat and gently warm over very low heat, stirring continuously until sauce thickens. Combine cheese sauce, cooked mushrooms, nutmeg, parsley and seasoning and mix well.

Remove the spinach from the oven once cooked. Carefully turn out upside down onto a sheet of greased baking paper. Spread the mushroom and cheese mixture over the spinach then roll up. Tightly wrap the roll in cling wrap, then refrigerate at least 2 hours before serving in slices.

Serves: 4
Total cooking time: 20 minutes preparation, 25 minutes cooking

Tofu balls with salad

Carbohydrate

Tofu balls

300g (9½ oz) hard tofu, roughly chopped

1 tablespoon fresh garlic chives, chopped

¼ teaspoon dried chilli flakes, or to taste

2 fresh kaffir lime leaves, finely shredded

1 stem lemon grass, white part only, sliced

½ teaspoon sea salt

Dressing

½ garlic clove, finely chopped

2 tablespoons lime juice

2 tablespoons tamari

2 tablespoons water

Salad

4 cups rocket leaves

2 small Lebanese cucumber, halved lengthways and
   sliced diagonally

½ red onion, thinly sliced

100g (3½ oz) grape tomatoes, halved

*Combine tofu, chives, chilli, lime leaves, lemongrass and seasoning
in a blender and process until smooth. Form tofu mixture into
2 cm (1 inch) diameter balls, place on a non-stick baking tray and
bake at 200°C (390°F) for 20 minutes.*

*For the salad dressing, combine garlic, lime juice, tamari and water,
then set aside.*

Combine salad ingredients, tofu balls and dressing, toss together well and serve.

Serves: 4
Total cooking time: 10 minutes preparation, 20 minutes cooking

Radicchio and feta rolls

Protein

You can refrigerate these rolls once you have cooked them, and keep them handy for a packed lunch or as a snack throughout the day.

200g (7 oz) feta, crumbled

2 tablespoons Parmesan cheese, grated

2 cups of baby English spinach leaves

2 tablespoons fresh flat-leaf parsley leaves

1 tablespoon fresh oregano leaves, finely chopped

Freshly ground black pepper to taste

12 large radicchio lettuce leaves

Combine feta, Parmesan cheese, spinach, parsley, oregano and pepper. Wrap feta and Parmesan cheese mixture in the radicchio leaves and secure with toothpicks or skewers. Cook the radicchio rolls for 2 minutes each side on an oiled barbecue plate.

Makes: 12 roll-ups
Total cooking time: 10 minutes preparation, 6 minutes cooking

Fish fillets wrapped in vine leaves with saffron, leeks and parsley

Protein

3 tablespoons butter

2 tablespoons olive oil

3 leeks, thinly sliced

12 saffron threads

½ cup fresh flat-leaf parsley leaves, chopped

32 large vine leaves in brine, drained

8 white fish fillets

Sea salt and freshly ground black pepper

In a frying pan melt butter, add olive oil, leeks and saffron and gently fry until leeks are softened; stir through parsley.

Wrap each fish fillet in 4 vine leaves with the saffron, leeks, parsley and seasoning. Secure parcels with twine if required. Place fish parcels on a baking tray and bake at 180°C (350°F) for 15 minutes or until fish are just cooked through.

Keep refrigerated; eat hot or cold.

Serves: 4
Total cooking time: 10 minutes preparation, 20 minutes cooking

Cajun spiced basmati rice salad with tomatoes, red kidney beans and fresh herbs

Carbohydrate

1 cup basmati rice

1 green capsicum, seeded and chopped

1 red capsicum, seeded and chopped

1 red onion, finely chopped

1 long red chilli, seeded and finely chopped

2 large tomatoes, chopped

420g (15 oz) canned red kidney beans, rinsed and
    drained

1 tablespoon fresh basil leaves, chopped

2 teaspoons fresh thyme leaves, chopped

1 teaspoon Cajun spice, or to taste

Salt and pepper

Fresh basil leaves, to garnish

Cook the rice in lightly salted water until just tender. Rinse with cold water and drain well. To a hot frying pan add capsicum, onion and 1 tablespoon of water, then cook until vegetables soften. Add the chilli and tomatoes, and cook for a further 2 minutes. Add the vegetable mixture and red kidney beans to the rice. Stir well to combine thoroughly.

Stir the chopped herbs and Cajun spice into the rice mixture. Season to taste with salt and pepper, and serve, garnished with basil leaves.

Serves: 4

Total cooking time: 5 minutes preparation, 30 minutes cooking

Feta, sun-dried tomato and prosciutto rolls with rocket salad

Protein

Feta, sun-dried tomato and prosciutto rolls

12 slices of prosciutto

12 semi sun-dried tomatoes

12 thin slices of feta

1 teaspoon oregano

Rocket salad

4 cups rocket leaves

2 tablespoons olive oil

1 tablespoon white wine vinegar

1 tablespoon fresh mint, finely chopped

Sea salt and freshly cracked black pepper to taste

For the prosciutto rolls, place one tomato and one piece of feta on each slice of prosciutto; scatter over a little of the oregano and roll the tomato and feta up in the prosciutto.

For the rocket salad, combine all ingredients and toss well.

Serve salad with the prosciutto rolls.

Serves: 2–3
Total cooking time: 5 minutes preparation

Salad with sumac

Protein

1 red onion, finely diced

1 teaspoon sumac

Juice of 2 lemons

2 garlic cloves, crushed

½ cup olive oil

1 baby cos lettuce, shredded

1 red capsicum, seeded, halved and sliced

1 green capsicum, seeded, halved and sliced

4 tomatoes, diced

2 Lebanese cucumber, sliced

1 cup fresh flat-leaf parsley leaves, chopped

Sea salt and freshly cracked black pepper to taste

Combine all ingredients together, toss well.

Serves: 2–3
Total cooking time: 5 minutes preparation

Omelette with salmon, sour cream and fresh herbs

Protein

100g (3½ oz) smoked salmon, chopped

3 tablespoons sour cream

2 tablespoons fresh dill, chopped

12 eggs, lightly beaten

1 tablespoon fresh chives, chopped

½ teaspoon sea salt

½ teaspoon freshly ground black pepper

2 tablespoons butter

4 sprigs fresh dill, extra, to garnish

Combine salmon, sour cream and chives and set aside.

Combine eggs, seasoning and chives. Heat 1 teaspoon of the butter in a large frying pan; add a quarter of the egg mixture and cook over medium heat for 4 minutes. Top omelette with a quarter of the salmon mixture, fold the omelette in half to enclose the salmon mixture.
Repeat with remaining ingredients to form 4 omelettes.
Garnish with extra dill and serve.

Serves: 4
Total cooking time: 5 minutes preparation, 15 minutes cooking

Roasted Lebanese eggplant with capsicum, feta and rocket

Protein

10 Lebanese eggplants

2 medium red capsicums

2 tablespoons olive oil

1 tablespoon lemon juice

Sea salt and freshly cracked black pepper, to taste

200g (7 oz) feta cheese

Small bunch of rocket leaves

Place the eggplants and capsicum in the oven at 200°C (390°F) for 20 minutes or until eggplants are tender and capsicum skin has blackened and blistered. Remove eggplant from the oven and allow to cool. Place capsicum in a plastic bag and allow to cool; once cooled peel, seed and slice lengthwise into 1 cm (½ inch) wide strips.

Slice the eggplant in half lengthwise without cutting all the way through. Combine oil, lemon juice and seasoning; baste both inside halves of the eggplant with the dressing. Place a strip of capsicum along the bottom of each eggplant, top with the feta and rocket leaves. Sandwich the eggplant halves back together and place in the refrigerator for 2 hours before serving.

Makes: 10
Total cooking time: 20 minutes cooking, 10 minutes preparation

Radicchio and rocket salad with cherry tomatoes, prosciutto and Parmesan cheese

Protein

150g (5 oz) cherry tomatoes, halved

2 Lebanese cucumbers, sliced

1 red capsicum, seeded and sliced

1 raddichio, leaves torn

3 cups rocket leaves

100g (3½ oz) thinly sliced prosciutto, chopped

100g (3½ oz) shaved Parmesan cheese

2 garlic cloves, crushed

3 tablespoons fresh basil leaves, shredded

3 tablespoons olive oil

Juice of ½ a lemon

Sea salt and freshly cracked black pepper to taste

Combine all ingredients together in a large salad bowl, toss well and serve.

Serves: 2–3
Total cooking time: 15 minutes preparation

Burghul and chickpea salad with mandarins

Carbohydrate

250g (8 oz) burghul, soaked in water overnight

400g (14 oz) canned chickpeas, drained and rinsed

3 mandarins, peeled and broken into wedges

Juice of ½ lemon

1 tablespoon ground cumin

1 teaspoon ground cinnamon

½ cup fresh flat-leaf parsley leaves, chopped

Sea salt and freshly ground black pepper to taste

Drain and squeeze any excess moisture from the burghul and place in a bowl. Add the remaining ingredients and toss to combine. Season to taste.

Serves: 4
Total cooking time: 12 hours soaking, 5 minutes preparation

Lamb and vegetable kebabs

Protein

600g (20 oz) diced lamb steak

2 zucchinis, sliced thickly on the diagonal

2 red onions, peeled, ends left intact and cut into wedges

2 red capsicums, seeded and cut into eighths

½ cup olive oil

2 tablespoons lemon juice

2 cloves of garlic, crushed

2 tablespoons fresh mint, finely chopped

1 teaspoon fresh rosemary, finely chopped

½ teaspoon freshly cracked black pepper

Salt to taste

Leave skewers to soak overnight to avoid burning on the barbecue.
Thread skewers with the lamb, zucchini, onion and capsicum.
Combine all other ingredients. Pour the marinade mixture over the
lamb skewers; cover and refrigerate 2–3 hours. Remove from fridge
and barbecue over a hot grill for 10 minutes or until meat is
cooked through.

Keep refrigerated for lunches; reheat or eat cold.

Serves: 4
Total cooking time: 2–3 hours marinating, 10 minutes preparation,
10 minutes cooking

Smoked salmon, caper, tarragon and dill muffins

Protein

Salmon muffins are one of my favourites because they are so versatile; great for snacks, lunches or entrées. Keep them refrigerated or frozen for an easily accessible quick bite.

100g (3½ oz) smoked salmon

½ cup fresh dill

¼ cup fresh tarragon

2 tablespoons capers

5 eggs

150g (5 oz) mascarpone cheese

Freshly cracked black pepper to taste

Combine all ingredients in a blender until well processed; herbs and salmon should appear minced. Pour mixture into greased muffin tins. Bake at 200°C (390°F) for 20 minutes. Serve hot or cold.

Makes: 12
Total cooking time: 5 minutes preparation, 20 minutes cooking

Risotto with artichoke and fennel

Carbohydrate

I always make a big batch of this recipe and refrigerate or freeze it for lunches and late dinners.

1 red onion, thinly sliced
1 fennel bulb, thinly sliced
2 cups basmati rice
400g (14 oz) canned artichoke hearts, drained and
    quartered
8 cups vegetable stock
Juice and zest of 1 lemon
2 tablespoons white wine vinegar
2 tablespoons fresh oregano, chopped
¼ cup fresh flat-leaf parsley leaves, chopped
Sea salt and freshly cracked black pepper to taste

Sauté onion and fennel with ¼ cup of water in a large non-stick frying pan for 8 minutes. Add basmati rice and artichokes, then stir-fry for 2 minutes. Add lemon juice and zest, and vinegar and 1 cup of the vegetable stock; cook stirring continuously until fluid is absorbed. Continue adding vegetable stock, 1 cup at a time. The amount of stock needed may vary so use less or more stock as required until rice is cooked. Stir through oregano, parsley and seasoning.

Serves: 4
Total cooking time: 5 minutes preparation, 25 minutes cooking

Asian prawn salad with chilli and lime dressing

Protein

Vietnamese mint has narrow, pointed leaves with distinctive dark markings in the middle of each leaf. It is not really a mint variety, however this is its common name. You will easily acquire this herb at an Asian grocery store; substitute with normal mint if necessary.

400g (14 oz) large cooked prawns, shelled and deveined
5 cups rocket
½ cup coriander, leaves, chopped
¼ cup Vietnamese mint, chopped
2 Lebanese cucumbers, thinly sliced
150g (5 oz) grape tomatoes, halved

Chilli and lime dressing
2 tablespoons peanut oil
1 teaspoon sesame oil
2 tablespoons vinegar
1 garlic clove, crushed
1 long red chilli, seeded and chopped
½ teaspoon shrimp paste
Sea salt and freshly cracked black pepper to taste

Combine prawns, rocket, coriander, mint, cucumber and tomatoes.

For the dressing, combine all ingredients in a jar, shake well then pour over salad. Toss salad well to combine.

Serves: 4
Total cooking time: 5 minutes preparation

Baked ricotta tarts with roast tomatoes and basil

Protein

Another versatile food suitable for snacks, lunches or entrées. Keep refrigerated for food emergencies.

6 Roma tomatoes, cut in half lengthways

2 tablespoons olive oil

Sea salt and freshly cracked black pepper

12 fresh basil leaves

500g (16 oz) fresh ricotta

1 egg, lightly beaten

¼ cup fresh flat-leaf parsley leaves, chopped

1 garlic clove, crushed

¼ teaspoon sea salt

¼ teaspoon freshly cracked pepper

Place tomatoes on a baking tray, then drizzle with olive oil and season. Bake tomatoes at 180°C (350°F) for 25 minutes.

Combine ricotta, egg, parsley, garlic, salt and pepper. Mix well, then spoon mixture into greased muffin tins. Bake at 180°C (350°F) for 20 minutes. Once cooked allow to cool slightly before gently turning out onto a rack. To serve top each tart with a roasted tomato half and one fresh basil leaf. Serve tarts warm or cold.

Makes: 12

Total cooking time: 5 minutes preparation, 25 minutes cooking

Vegetarian meals

Red capsicum frittata with parsley and Parmesan cheese

Sweet potato bake with tomatoes and crunchy Performax topping

Radish and tomato soup with cucumber

Vegetarian omelette with tarragon and capers

Asian-style braised vegetables

Vegetable risotto

Curried mushrooms served with chilli beans

Vegetarian san choy bow

Spicy sour soup with tofu, mushroom and bok choy

Cauliflower and broccoli soup with Gruyere cheese

Tofu skewers with lemon and fresh herb marinade served with
grilled tomatoes

Red lentil and basmati rice casserole with vegetables and spices

Spinach and parsley soup with mascarpone cheese

Spicy tomato and chickpeas with saffron-flavoured doongara rice

Avocado and tomato salsa with barbecued vegetables

Grilled haloumi, tomato and eggplant salad

Barley tabouleh with preserved lemon

Burghul salad with sun-dried tomatoes, cucumber, parsley
and mint

Zucchini and tomato curry with coriander and fenugreek served
with saffron rice

Lentil salad with chilli, capsicum and celery

Vegetable stir-fry

Artichoke soup

Chickpea salad

Red capsicum frittata with parsley and Parmesan cheese

Protein

¼ cup olive oil

1 red onion, finely chopped

2 red capsicums, seeded and chopped

6 eggs, lightly beaten

½ cup cream

¼ cup flat-leaf parsley, chopped

Sea salt and freshly ground pepper to taste

¼ cup Parmesan cheese, grated

Heat oil in a large frying pan, add the onion and cook for 2 minutes, add the capsicum and cook for 10 minutes or until softened.

Combine eggs, cream, parsley and seasoning; pour egg mixture over the capsicum and onions. Cook frittata over low heat for 20 minutes; sprinkle with Parmesan cheese then place under a hot grill for 4 minutes or until golden brown. Serve with suitable protein style side-salad.

Serves: 4
Total cooking time: 5 minutes preparation, 30 minutes cooking

Sweet potato bake with tomatoes and crunchy Performax topping

Carbohydrate

This recipe uses dried breadcrumbs. It is important that the bread you use has a GI of less than 50 with minimal fat content. I use Performax bread by Country Life Bakeries which is an Australian brand that has a GI of 38.

2 large sweet potatoes, peeled, sliced, rinsed and drained
800g (28 oz) canned diced tomatoes
1 onion, finely chopped
½ cup fresh basil, shredded
1 garlic clove, crushed
Sea salt and freshly cracked black pepper to taste
3 cups dried bread crumbs, made from Performax bread
　　or equivalent
1½ tablespoons mixed dried herbs
1 tablespoon ground cumin
1 teaspoon sea salt
½ teaspoon freshly cracked black pepper

Cook potato slices in boiling salted water until just tender and cooked through; drain.

In a large frying pan sauté onion and garlic with 1 tablespoon of water until just softened. Add tomatoes, basil and seasoning; bring to the boil then allow to simmer five minutes.

Layer the bottom of a casserole dish with the potato slices, top with tomato and onion mixture. Combine bread crumbs, mixed herbs, cumin, salt and pepper; sprinkle mixture over the potatoes and tomatoes. Bake at 180°C (350°F) for 20 minutes.

Serves: 6–8
Total cooking time: 10 minutes preparation, 30 minutes cooking

Radish and tomato soup with cucumber

Protein

1 tablespoon olive oil

1 garlic clove, crushed

1 small red onion, finely chopped

150g (5 oz) radish, trimmed and chopped

400g (14 oz) canned diced tomatoes

1 cup vegetable stock

Sea salt and freshly cracked black pepper to taste

2 Lebanese cucumbers, halved, seeded and diced

¼ cup fresh basil leaves, chopped

Heat oil in a frying pan and sauté garlic and onion until onion softens.

Place onion, radish, tomatoes and stock in a processor and blend until smooth, then season to taste. Refrigerate soup 3 hours or until chilled, then pour into 4 bowls and top with cucumber and basil.

Serves: 4
Total cooking time: 10 minutes preparation, 3 hours refrigeration

Vegetarian omelette with tarragon and capers

Protein

2 tablespoons olive oil

1 onion, finely chopped

100g (3½ oz) green snake beans, trimmed and cut into
    5 cm (2 inch) lengths

6 asparagus spears, trimmed and quartered

2 baby yellow squash, halved and sliced

6 eggs, lightly beaten

2 tablespoons cream

½ cup grated cheese

1 tablespoon fresh tarragon leaves, chopped

1 tablespoon capers, chopped

2 tablespoons fresh flat-leaf parsley leaves, chopped

Sea salt and freshly ground black pepper to taste

Heat oil in a large frying pan, add onions and cook until soft. Add beans, asparagus and squash, and stir-fry for 6 minutes or until vegetables are tender and cooked through. Combine eggs, cream, cheese, tarragon, capers, parsley and seasoning. Pour egg mixture over the vegetables and fork through. Cook omelette for 8 minutes over medium heat, then place under a grill and cook for a further 5 minutes or until browned and set. Cut into wedges and serve garnished with extra sprigs of parsley.

Serves: 4
Total cooking time: 5 minutes preparation, 20 minutes cooking

Asian-style braised vegetables

Protein

4 tablespoons peanut oil

2 teaspoons sesame oil

4 spring onions, sliced

1 garlic clove, crushed

6 button mushrooms, quartered

6 oyster mushrooms

150g (5 oz) green snake beans, trimmed and cut into
    5 cm (2 inch) lengths

200g (7 oz) broccoli cut into florets

8 asparagus spears, trimmed and quartered

2 tablespoons almond slivers

4 baby bok choy, quartered

2 tablespoons fresh coriander leaves, chopped

2 tablespoons fresh Thai basil leaves, chopped

Sea salt and freshly cracked black pepper to taste

Heat oils in a large wok, add onions, garlic, mushrooms, beans, broccoli, asparagus, almonds and bok choy; stir-fry for 8 minutes or until vegetables are tender and cooked through. Stir through coriander, basil and seasoning and serve.

Serves: 4
Total cooking time: 10 minutes preparation, 10 minutes cooking

Vegetable risotto

Carbohydrate

1 leek, sliced

1 zucchini, sliced

½ cup peas

100g (3½ oz) green snake beans, trimmed and cut into
  5 cm (2 inch) lengths

1 head broccoli, cut into small florets

2 cups basmati rice

8 cups vegetable stock

½ cup fresh flat-leaf parsley leaves, chopped

Sea salt and freshly cracked black pepper to taste

In a large non-stick frying pan sauté leek and garlic with ¼ cup of water until leek softens. Add zucchini, peas, beans, broccoli and ½ a cup of water; stir-fry 6 minutes. Add rice and stir-fry a further minute. Add one cup of the vegetable stock, stir-fry until all fluid is absorbed. Continue adding 1 cup of stock at a time. The amount of stock needed may vary so use less or more stock as required until rice is cooked. Stir through parsley and seasoning.

Serves: 4–6
Total cooking time: 5 minutes preparation, 30 minutes cooking

Curried mushrooms served with chilli beans

Protein

Curried mushrooms

2 tablespoons olive oil

1 onion, thinly sliced

1 garlic clove, crushed

2 tablespoons butter

500g (16 oz) mushrooms sliced

¼ teaspoon dried chilli flakes, or to taste

1 tablespoon mild curry powder

400g (14 oz) canned diced tomatoes

2 tablespoons sour cream

½ cup fresh coriander leaves, chopped

Sea salt and freshly cracked black pepper to taste

Chilli beans

1 tablespoons olive oil

200g (7 oz) green snake beans, trimmed

1 red onion, thinly sliced

¼ teaspoon cayenne pepper

Sea salt and freshly cracked black pepper to taste

Heat oil in a large frying pan, add onions and garlic and cook until onion is softened. Add butter, mushrooms, chilli and curry powder, then stir-fry for 5 minutes. Add tomatoes and cook for a further 5 minutes. Stir through cream, coriander and seasoning.

For the chilli beans, heat oil in a frying pan, add beans, onion and cayenne pepper and stir-fry for 5 minutes.

Serve mushrooms with beans to the side.

Serves: 4
Total cooking time: 5 minutes preparation, 20 minutes cooking

Vegetarian san choy bow
Protein/ Carbohydrate

This meal is made entirely from very low GI food or good carbohydrates. It is therefore suitable as either a protein or carbohydrate-style meal. It is also great served with grated cheese on top; adding the cheese would of course make the meal a protein-only style meal.

4 spring onions, thinly sliced
1 garlic clove, crushed
20 button mushrooms, finely chopped
4 tablespoons tomato paste
8 semi sun-dried tomatoes, finely chopped
3 cups wom bok, finely chopped
2 cups bean shoots
½ teaspoon sambal oelek, or to taste
Juice of ½ lemon
¼ cup fresh Vietnamese mint leaves, finely chopped
½ cup fresh coriander leaves, finely chopped
Sea salt and freshly cracked black pepper to taste
1 iceberg lettuce, halved

In a large wok cook spring onions and garlic with ¼ cup of water until onion softens. Add the mushrooms and fry for 5 minutes. Add the tomato paste, sun-dried tomatoes, wom bok, bean shoots and sambal oelek, then stir-fry for 5 minutes. Stir through lemon juice, mint, coriander and seasoning. Serve mushroom mixture in lettuce cups.

Serves: 4
Total cooking time: 5 minutes preparation, 15 minutes cooking

Spicy sour soup with tofu, mushroom and bok choy

Carbohydrate

4 cups vegetable stock

1 teaspoon ginger, freshly grated

1 fresh lemongrass stem, white part thinly sliced

4 kaffir lime leaves, thinly sliced

1 birds-eye chilli, seeded and finely chopped

8 button mushrooms, halved

100g (3½ oz) silken firm tofu, cut into 1.5 cm (½ inch)
   cubes

3 baby bok choy, roughly chopped

Juice of 1 lime

2 tablespoons fresh coriander leaves, chopped

Sea salt to taste

In a large saucepan bring stock to the boil, then add the ginger, lemongrass, lime leaves and chilli. Reduce heat and simmer for 5 minutes covered. Next add mushrooms and tofu, then simmer a further five minutes; add bok choy and simmer until wilted. Remove from heat, then add lime juice, coriander and salt to taste. Serve hot into bowls.

Serves: 4

Total cooking time: 5 minutes preparation, 12 minutes cooking

Cauliflower and broccoli soup with Gruyere cheese

Protein

This is a delicious soup. The Gruyere cheese creates a wonderful creamy texture. I usually freeze this soup in single serves for an instant reheatable meal for one.

1 tablespoon olive oil

1 red onion, finely chopped

2 garlic cloves, crushed

1 head cauliflower, broken into florets

1 head broccoli, broken into florets

4 cups vegetable stock

100g (3½ oz) Gruyere cheese, crumbled

½ teaspoon paprika

½ cup cream

¼ teaspoon freshly cracked black pepper

Paprika and Gruyere cheese shavings, extra to garnish

Heat oil in a large saucepan, add the onion and garlic and cook until onion softens. Add the cauliflower, broccoli and stock; bring to the boil then reduce heat and allow to simmer for 15 minutes, or until vegetables are soft. Place soup in a blender and process until smooth. Return soup to the saucepan, then add the cheese, paprika, cream and pepper. Gently warm soup, then serve into bowls garnished with the extra paprika and cheese.

Serves: 4–6

Total cooking time: 5 minutes preparation, 20 minutes cooking

Tofu skewers with lemon and fresh herb marinade served with grilled tomatoes

Carbohydrate

350g (12 oz) firm tofu, drained and cut into 2 cm (1 inch) squares

1 red capsicum, seeded and cut into 2 cm (1 inch) pieces

1 yellow capsicum, seeded and cut into 2 cm (1 inch) pieces

2 zucchinis, cut into 2 cm (1 inch) chunks

8 small button mushrooms, halved

slices of lemon, to garnish

grated rind and juice of lemon

1 garlic clove, crushed

1 teaspoon fresh rosemary, chopped

1 teaspoon fresh thyme, chopped

½ teaspoon salt

½ teaspoon pepper

4 large tomatoes, halved

Blanch capsicum and zucchini in boiling salted water; drain. Thread alternating capsicum, zucchini, mushrooms and tofu onto skewers. Combine lemon zest and juice, garlic, rosemary, thyme and seasoning. Baste skewers and tomato halves with the marinade. Grill skewers and tomatoes for 10 minutes under a hot grill, turning skewers frequently and basting with the marinade. Serve skewers with tomatoes to the side.

Makes: 12
Total cooking time: 30 minutes marinating, 5 minutes preparation,
10 minutes cooking

Red lentil and basmati rice casserole with vegetables and spices

Carbohydrate

1 cup red lentils

½ cup basmati rice

5 cups vegetable stock

1 leek, sliced

1 red capsicum, seeded and sliced

½ head of broccoli, florets

100g (3½ oz) green beans, trimmed and cut into
    5 cm (2 inch) lengths

400g (14 oz) canned chopped tomatoes

2 garlic cloves, crushed

1 teaspoon ground cumin

1 teaspoon chilli powder

1 teaspoon garam masala

2 tablespoons fresh basil, chopped

Sea salt and freshly cracked black pepper to taste

Fresh basil sprigs, extra to garnish

Place the lentils, rice and vegetable stock in a large saucepan; bring to boil then simmer, stirring occasionally, for 20 minutes. Add all other ingredients, cover saucepan and simmer for a further 15 minutes, or until vegetables are tender. Season as required and serve in bowls garnished with sprigs of fresh basil.

Serves: 4

Total cooking time: 5 minutes preparation, 35 minutes cooking

Spinach and parsley soup with mascarpone cheese

Protein

1 tablespoon olive oil

2 tablespoons butter

6 spring onions, sliced

2 sticks of celery, chopped

6 cups vegetable stock

500g (16 oz) fresh spinach leaves

½ cup fresh flat-leaf parsley leaves

100g (3½ oz) mascarpone cheese

Sea salt and freshly cracked black pepper to taste

Heat oil and butter in a large saucepan, add onions and celery and cook until onion softens. Add stock, spinach leaves and parsley; cover, then bring to the boil; reduce heat and allow to simmer for 20 minutes. Process soup in a blender until smooth then return to the saucepan. Stir through the cheese and seasoning. Gently reheat then serve.

Serves: 4

Total cooking time: 5 minutes preparation, 30 minutes cooking

Spicy tomato and chickpeas with saffron flavoured doongara rice

Carbohydrate

Doongara is a type of rice with a moderate GI. You can substitute Doongara with basmati rice if necessary.

2 brown onions, chopped

1 garlic clove, crushed

1 tablespoon ground cumin

1 teaspoon paprika

¼ teaspoon dried chilli flakes, or to taste

800g (28 oz) canned chopped tomatoes

800g (28 oz) canned chickpeas, rinsed and drained

½ cup fresh coriander leaves, chopped

¼ cup fresh flat-leaf parsley, chopped

Sea salt and freshly cracked black pepper to taste

12 saffron threads

1 cup doongara rice (or basmati rice)

To a large saucepan add onions and garlic with 2 tablespoons of water and gently stir-fry until onions become translucent. Add cumin, paprika and chilli and stir-fry a further minute. Add tomatoes and chickpeas; bring to the boil; reduce heat and simmer for 15 minutes or until mixture has thickened. Stir through coriander, parsley and seasoning.

For saffron rice, cook rice in the usual method with the saffron. Serve chickpea and tomato mixture with the rice.

Serve: 4

Total cooking time: 5 minutes preparation, 30 minutes cooking

Avocado and tomato salsa with barbecued vegetables

Protein

Avocado and tomato salsa

1 avocado, diced

2 tomatoes, seeded and diced

½ red capsicum, diced

½ yellow capsicum, diced

1 Lebanese cucumber, diced

2 tablespoons fresh coriander, chopped

2 tablespoons fresh flat-leaf parsley, chopped

½ birds-eye chilli, seeded and finely chopped

Juice of ½ lemon

Sea salt and freshly cracked black pepper to taste

Barbecued vegetables

2 eggplants, sliced 1 cm (½ inch) thick lengthways

Salt

2 garlic cloves, crushed

2 tablespoons fresh mint, chopped

¼ cup olive oil

¼ teaspoon sea salt

¼ teaspoon freshly cracked black pepper

16 asparagus spears

4 zucchinis, halved and sliced 1 cm (½ inch) thick
    lengthways

4 baby yellow squash, sliced 1 cm (½ inch) thick

For the avocado and tomato salsa, combine all ingredients together, mix well and season with salt and pepper.

For the barbecued vegetables, place sliced eggplant on a tray and sprinkle liberally with salt. Allow to sit 30 minutes; rinse then pat dry. Combine garlic, mint, olive oil, salt and pepper. Baste vegetables liberally with the olive oil mixture. Cook vegetables on a barbecue for 3–5 minutes each side, basting frequently with the marinade, until tender and cooked through.

Serve vegetables with avocado and tomato salsa on top.

Serves: 4
Total cooking time: 10 minutes preparation, 30 minutes standing,
10 minutes cooking

Grilled haloumi, tomato and eggplant salad
Protein

Haloumi is a Greek-style cheese that is quite salty in flavour and easily crumbles. It is available in my local supermarket so you should easily be able to find it at your supermarket or at your local delicatessen.

¼ cup olive oil

1 garlic clove, crushed

4 Lebanese eggplants, halved lengthways

4 Roma tomatoes, halved lengthways

400g (14 oz) haloumi cheese, sliced thinly

6 cups rocket, chopped coarsely

2 tablespoons fresh basil leaves, chopped

2 tablespoons red wine vinegar

1 tablespoon drained capers, chopped

Combine oil and garlic, then baste eggplants, tomatoes and haloumi. Grill vegetables and cheese on a barbecue hot plate for 3–5 minutes each side, basting frequently with the oil, until browned and cooked through. Allow vegetables and cheese to cool slightly before combining with rocket, basil, vinegar, capers, seasoning and any remaining oil. Toss well and serve.

Serves: 4
Total cooking time: 5 minutes preparation, 10 minutes cooking

Barley tabouleh with preserved lemon

Carbohydrate

2 cups pearl barley

Juice of 2 lemons

¼ cup white wine vinegar

2 tablespoons preserved lemon, finely sliced

1 tablespoon ground cumin

1 tablespoon sea salt

1 cup fresh flat-leaf parsley leaves, chopped

1 cup watercress sprigs

1 red Spanish onion, finely chopped

2 celery hearts, thinly sliced

½ cup fresh coriander leaves, chopped

Freshly cracked black pepper to taste

Cook barley in boiling water for 1 hour; drain then add all other ingredients and mix well.

Serves: 4
Total cooking time: 10 minutes preparation, 1 hour cooking

Burghul salad with sun-dried tomatoes, cucumber, parsley and mint

Carbohydrate

Burghul, also spelt 'bulgur', is made from whole wheat that has been soaked and baked to make cooking quicker. Burghul comes either whole or cracked. This recipe calls for cracked burghul.

1 cup cracked burghul

50g (1½ oz) sun-dried tomatoes, sliced thinly (do *not* use tomatoes that are in oil)

2 Lebanese cucumbers, peeled, halved, deseeded and chopped

½ cup fresh flat-leaf parsley leaves, chopped

2 tablespoons fresh mint leaves, chopped

Sea salt and freshly cracked black pepper to taste

Juice and zest of 1 lemon

1 tablespoon ground cumin

Place burghul in a large bowl, pour over 1 cup of boiling water and leave to stand for 30 minutes. Drain and allow to cool before mixing through all other ingredients.

Serves: 4

Total cooking time: 5 minutes preparation, 30 minutes soaking

Zucchini and tomato curry with coriander and fenugreek

Protein

2 tablespoons vegetable oil

1 onion, finely chopped

3 fresh long green chillies, finely chopped

2 teaspoons fenugreek seeds

1 teaspoon ginger, freshly grated

1 garlic clove, crushed

1 teaspoon chilli powder, or to taste

2 teaspoons curry powder

6 zucchinis, thinly sliced

3 baby yellow squash, thinly sliced

800g (28 oz) canned diced tomatoes

2 tablespoons fresh coriander leaves, chopped

Sea salt and freshly cracked black pepper to taste

Fresh coriander leaves, extra to garnish

Heat the oil in a frying pan; add the onion, chillies, fenugreek seeds, ginger, garlic, chilli powder and curry powder, then stir-fry until onion softens. Add zucchini and squash, then stir-fry 5 minutes or until vegetables are tender and cooked through. Add tomatoes and cook for 5 minutes or until fluid has condensed. Stir-through coriander and seasoning. Serve garnished with extra coriander leaves.

Serves: 4
Total cooking time: 5 minutes preparation, 15 minutes cooking

Lentil salad with chilli, capsicum and celery

Carbohydrate

1 brown onion, finely chopped

400g (14 oz) brown lentils, soaked overnight, drained
   and rinsed

1 cup hot vegetable stock

½ red capsicum, seeded and finely chopped

½ green capsicum, seeded and finely chopped

1 Lebanese cucumber, halved, seeded and chopped

2 celery stalks, peeled, finely diced

1 spring onion, sliced finely

1 fresh birds-eye chilli, seeded and finely chopped

2 tablespoons fresh flat-leaf parsley leaves, chopped

Juice of ½ lemon

Sea salt and freshly cracked black pepper to taste

In a large non-stick saucepan stir-fry the onion with a little water until it softens, add lentils and vegetable stock; simmer covered for approximately 20 minutes until all fluid is absorbed. Remove from heat and allow to cool. Once cooled add all other ingredients and mix well.

Serves: 4
Total cooking time: 5 minutes preparation, 20 minutes cooking

Vegetable stir-fry

Protein

1 tablespoon olive oil

2 tablespoons butter

1 onion, thinly sliced

2 sticks of celery, thinly sliced

1 fennel bulb, trimmed and thinly sliced

1 eggplant, peeled and cubed

200g (7 oz) green snake beans, trimmed and cut into
   5 cm (2 inch) lengths

1 head of broccoli, broken into florets and blanched

4 tomatoes, diced

2 tablespoons fresh oregano leaves, chopped

½ cup fresh flat-leaf parsley, chopped

Sea salt and freshly cracked black pepper to taste

Heat oil and butter in a large wok, add the onion and cook until softened. Add the celery, fennel, eggplant, beans, broccoli and tomatoes and stir-fry for 10 minutes. Stir through oregano, parsley and seasoning and serve.

Serves: 4
Total cooking time: 5 minutes preparation, 15 minutes cooking

Artichoke soup

Protein/Carbohydrate

This soup is suitable as a protein-style or a carbohydrate-style meal as it uses only good carbohydrates that have a very low GI. Make sure to remove any tough outer leaves on the artichokes before pureeing them.

1 onion, finely chopped

1 garlic clove, crushed

800g (28 oz) canned artichoke hearts, drained and
   chopped

5 cups vegetable stock

1 tablespoon fresh thyme leaves, chopped

4 sun-dried tomatoes, finely chopped

Sauté onion and garlic in a frying pan with 2 tablespoons of water until onion softens. In a blender process the cooked onion and garlic, artichokes and vegetable stock until well pureed. In a large saucepan bring soup to the boil; add the thyme and sun-dried tomatoes. Allow to simmer for 2 minutes then serve.

Serves: 4–6
Total cooking time: 5 minutes preparation, 10 minutes cooking

Chickpea salad
Carbohydrate

This salad is very quick and easy to prepare. You can serve it as a side-dish with a main meal or as a light lunch or snack between meals.

800g (28 oz) canned chickpeas, rinsed and drained

6 spring onions, trimmed and sliced lengthways

2 Lebanese cucumbers, halved, seeded and chopped

1 red capsicum, seeded and finely sliced

Juice of 1 lemon

2 teaspoons ground cumin

1 teaspoon turmeric

½ cup fresh flat-leaf parsley leaves, chopped

Sea salt and freshly cracked black pepper to taste

Combine all ingredients; season to taste with salt and freshly cracked black pepper.

Serves: 4
Total cooking time: 5 minutes preparation

Meals for two

Prawn and pork skewers with rosemary and anchovy marinade

Lamb cutlets with stir-fried vegetables and olive oil and
parsley dressing

Barramundi fillets with Thai flavours

Stuffed roast quail served with baby fennel and artichokes

Spinach and Parmesan cheese bake with ricotta and blue vein cheese

Chilli and thyme mushroooms served with pancetta and
avocado cream

Saganaki served with rocket

Egg crepes with chicken, tomato and spinach, drizzled with
garlic mayonnaise

Stir-fried spicy octopus served with avocado salsa

Steak with mushrooms, spring onions and anchovy and tarragon
butter with rocket salad

Snapper with chilli and lime served with spinach and cucumber salad

Coddled eggs and tarragon with grilled prosciutto

Lentil and lime soup with onion and coriander

Beef tenderloin with green pepper sauce served with asparagus
and bean salad

Lamb salad with lemon dressing

Fish fillets with walnut and lemon, served with squash and
asparagus stir-fry

Mixed mushroom omelette

Chicken and artichoke skewers served with mixed barbecued vegetables

Chicken burgers with basil and mint served with tomato
and feta salad

Pork steaks with tomato and tamarind sauce

Barbecued lamb cutlets served with rocket salad with feta
and walnuts
Swordfish with spicy macadamia and mint pesto served with
cucumber salad
Sardines wrapped in vine leaves with spiced garlic and almond butter
served with fennel, tomato and parsley salad
Stir-fried squid and bok choy

Prawn and pork skewers with rosemary and anchovy marinade

Protein

200g (7 oz) diced pork

200g (7 oz) prawn meat

8 bamboo skewers, pre-soaked

6 anchovy fillets

1 teaspoon fresh rosemary, finely chopped

¼ cup olive oil

1 teaspoon lemon juice

Sea salt and freshly ground black pepper to taste

Thread prawns and pork onto the bamboo skewers alternately. In a mortar, pound anchovies, rosemary, olive oil and lemon juice together to form a paste; season. Pour marinade over the prawn and pork skewers and refrigerate for 2 hours. Char-grill skewers on a barbecue grill for 6 minutes or until cooked through.

Serves: 2
Total cooking time: 10 minutes preparation, 2 hours marinating,
6 minutes cooking

Lamb cutlets with stir-fried vegetables and olive oil and parsley dressing

Protein

4 lamb cutlets

1 tablespoon butter

½ cauliflower head, broken into small florets

½ green capsicum, seeded and sliced

½ red capsicum, seeded and sliced

½ cucumber, sliced

1 spring onion, sliced

2 tablespoons olive oil

1 tablespoon white wine vinegar

2 tablespoons fresh flat-leaf parsley leaves, chopped

salt and freshly ground black pepper

For the cutlets barbecue or grill 3–4 minutes each side or until browned and cooked as desired. Season before serving.

For the vegetables, in a large saucepan melt butter; add cauliflower, capsicum, cucumber and onions and stir-fry 8 minutes or until just tender; set aside in a serving dish. Combine olive oil, vinegar, parsley and seasoning; mix well then pour dressing over the vegetables, tossing thoroughly to coat vegetables in dressing.

Serve cutlets with vegetables to the side.

Serves: 2
Total cooking time: 10 minutes preparation, 15 minutes cooking

Barramundi fillets with Thai flavours

Protein

2 kaffir lime leaves, thinly sliced

½ birds-eye chilli, seeded and finely chopped

1 tablespoon fresh lemongrass

1 tablespoon coriander leaves

½ teaspoon fish sauce

Juice of ½ lime

1 tablespoon peanut oil

2 barramundi fillets

2 cups baby spinach leaves

1 Lebanese cucumber, peeled into thin ribbons

Place each barramundi fillet on a piece of aluminium foil. Combine lime leaves, chilli, lemongrass, coriander, fish sauce, lime juice and peanut oil. Top each barramundi fillet with a quarter of the dressing, then fold aluminium foil around each fillet. Place in heated oven at 180°C (350°F) for 15 minutes or until just cooked through.

Divide spinach leaves and cucumber ribbons between 4 plates, top with the cooked barramundi and garnish with extra fresh coriander leaves.

Serves: 2

Total cooking time: 5 minutes preparation, 15 minutes cooking

Stuffed roast quail served with baby fennel and artichokes

Protein

Stuffed roast quail

1 tablespoon butter

1 tablespoon olive oil

100g (3½ oz) pancetta, chopped

½ red onion, finely chopped

50g (1½ oz) pork and veal mince

2 tablespoons flat-leaf parsley leaves, chopped

Sea salt and freshly cracked black pepper to taste

4 quails

2 tablespoons olive oil, extra

Baby fennel and artichokes

1 tablespoon olive oil

1 tablespoon butter

2 baby fennel bulbs, thinly sliced

3 canned artichoke hearts, halved

½ cup chicken stock

2 tablespoons white wine vinegar

1 teaspoon dried rosemary

1 teaspoon dried thyme

Sea salt and freshly cracked black pepper to taste

Fennel fronds reserved from the 2 baby fennel bulbs,
    chopped

*In a frying pan melt butter, add pancetta and onion and stir-fry
until onion has softened. Remove from heat and combine with mince,
parsley and seasoning.*

Divide the stuffing between the quails. Rub quails with olive oil and season before roasting at 220°C (420°F) for 12 minutes. Remove from oven and allow to rest in a warm place for 10 minutes before serving.

For the baby fennel and artichokes, heat oil and butter in a small saucepan, add the fennel and stir-fry over medium heat for 3 minutes. Add the artichokes, stock, vinegar, rosemary, thyme and seasoning. Cover; bring to the boil, then reduce heat and allow to simmer for 5 minutes. Remove lid and allow to simmer for a further 5 minutes. Stir through fennel fronds.

Serve the stuffed roast quail with baby fennel and artichokes to the side.

Serves: 2
Total cooking time: 10 minutes preparation, 15 minutes cooking,
10 minutes resting

Spinach and Parmesan cheese bake with ricotta and blue vein cheese

Protein

The flavour of the blue vein cheese in this recipe is very subtle, so do not be put off cooking this recipe if you do not normally eat blue vein cheese.

250g (8 oz) frozen spinach, thawed and squeezed of
  excess fluid

½ cup cream

3 egg yolks, lightly beaten

¼ teaspoon sea salt

Dash freshly ground black pepper

3 egg whites, stiffly beaten

3 eggs, separated

4 tablespoons grated Parmesan cheese

¼ teaspoon nutmeg

200g (7 oz) ricotta cheese

75g (2½ oz) blue vein cheese, finely chopped

Combine spinach, cream, egg yolks, Parmesan cheese and nutmeg in a large bowl; mix well. Gently fold egg whites into the spinach mixture. Spoon half the spinach mixture into a greased loaf tin.

Combine ricotta and blue vein cheese. Spoon cheese mixture over the top of the spinach mixture, then top with the remaining spinach mixture.

Bake at 180°C (350°F) for 25 minutes. Allow to cool slightly before gently remove from baking tin. Keep refrigerated, serve in slices hot or cold with salad leaves drizzled with olive oil to the side.

Serves: 4

Total cooking time: 15 minutes preparation, 25 minutes cooking

Chilli and thyme mushrooms served with pancetta and avocado cream

Protein

4 tablespoons olive oil

1 garlic clove, crushed

½ teaspoon dried chilli flakes

1 teaspoon dried thyme

4 large flat mushrooms, stalks removed

Sea salt and freshly cracked black pepper to taste

6 slices pancetta

½ avocado

1 tablespoon sour cream

1 teaspoon lemon juice

Combine oil, garlic, chilli and thyme; baste mushrooms with oil mixture, season then cook on the barbecue, basting frequently with olive oil mixture, for 5 minutes or until tender.

Grill pancetta on barbecue until golden brown, break into pieces.

Combine avocado, sour cream, lemon juice and season to taste. Serve mushrooms, topped with avocado mixture and pancetta pieces.

Serves: 4
Total cooking time: 5 minutes preparation, 5 minutes cooking

Saganaki served with rocket

Protein

Kefalograviera is a firm white Greek cheese that is traditionally fried to serve as this saganaki dish for a pre-dinner appetiser. I have found saganaki is also excellent for a light lunch or dinner.

2 triangles kefalograviera cheese

1 egg beaten

2 tablespoons olive oil

Fresh mint to garnish

Lemon wedges to serve

2 cups rocket

1 tablespoon olive oil

Baste kefalograviera with the egg. Heat oil in frying pan, fry cheese 1 minute each side over high heat, or until golden brown, serve with mint and lemon wedges. Serve rocket to the side, drizzled with olive oil.

Serves: 2
Total cooking time: 5 minutes

Egg crepes with chicken, tomato and spinach drizzled with garlic mayonnaise

Protein

Egg crepes

1 tablespoon olive oil

4 eggs, lightly beaten

½ red onion, thinly sliced

1 chicken breast fillet, cooked and diced

1 cup baby spinach leaves

1 tomato, diced

Garlic mayonnaise

1 tablespoon lemon juice

1 egg yolk

4 tablespoons olive oil

2 garlic cloves, crushed

Sea salt and freshly cracked black pepper to taste

Heat oil in a large frying pan. Pour half the egg mixture into the pan and cook for 2–3 minutes until set. Repeat with remaining mixture. Place each crepe on a plate, top with the onion, chicken, spinach leaves and tomato.

For the garlic mayonnaise, combine lemon juice and egg yolk, and beat well, then gradually add the olive oil. Add garlic and seasoning. Pour mayonnaise over the crepe filling then roll up the crepes and serve.

Serves: 2

Total cooking time: 10 minutes preparation, 15 minutes cooking

Stir-fried spicy octopus served with avocado salsa

Protein

Stir-fry spicy octopus
1 tablespoon olive oil

½ red onion, finely chopped

1 garlic clove, crushed

400g (14 oz) baby octopus

½ teaspoon paprika

pinch ground cayenne pepper, or as per taste

Juice of ½ lemon

¼ cup fresh flat-leaf parsley leaves, chopped

Sea salt and freshly cracked black pepper to taste

Avocado salsa
2 tomatoes, seeded and chopped finely

½ red onion, finely chopped

½ avocado, finely chopped

2 tablespoons fresh oregano leaves, finely chopped

2 tablespoons olive oil

Juice of ½ lemon

1 tablespoon apple cider vinegar

Sea salt and freshly cracked black pepper to taste

Heat oil in a large wok, add onion and garlic, then stir-fry until onion softens. Add octopus, paprika and cayenne, then stir-fry 6 minutes or until octopus is tender and cooked through. Stir through lemon juice, parsley and seasoning.

For the salsa, combine all ingredients together, mix well.

Serve octopus with salsa to the side.

Serves: 2

Total cooking time: 10 minutes preparation, 10 minutes cooking

Steaks with mushrooms, spring onions and anchovy and tarragon butter with rocket salad

Protein

2 sirloin steaks

2 flat mushrooms, peeled and stalks trimmed

4 spring onions, trimmed and cut into 10 cm (4 inches)
   lengths

4 tablespoons olive oil

Sea salt and freshly cracked black pepper to taste

Anchovy and tarragon butter

2 tablespoons butter

2 anchovy fillets, finely chopped

1 teaspoon fresh tarragon, finely chopped

1 teaspoon lemon juice

Sea salt and freshly cracked black pepper, to taste

Rocket salad

2 cups rocket

1 tablespoon olive oil

Baste steaks, mushrooms and onions with the oil, then season. Cook on the barbecue for 2–3 minutes each side. Leave steaks to rest in a warm place for 10 minutes before serving.

For the anchovy and tarragon butter, combine all ingredients together in a food processor until smooth.

Serve steaks onto a plate with mushrooms and onions to the side, place a dollop of the anchovy butter on each steak. Serve rocket salad to the side, drizzled with the olive oil.

Serves: 2

Total cooking time: 5 minutes preparation, 16 minutes cooking

166

Snapper with chilli and lime served with spinach and cucumber salad
Protein

When buying whole fish look for the following signs of freshness: moist and evenly slippery skin; moist and bright red gills; firm flesh that bounces back when touched; clear eyes; and a fresh smell.

Snapper with chilli and lime
1 birds-eye chilli, finely chopped

Juice and rind of 1 lime

2 tablespoons fresh coriander leaves, chopped

2 fresh kaffir lime leaves, shredded

1 stick of lemongrass, sliced

1 tablespoon fresh ginger, grated

3 spring onions, thinly sliced

2 tablespoons fish sauce

1 tablespoon sesame oil

2 whole snapper

Spinach and cucumber salad
100g (3½ oz) baby English spinach leaves

1 Lebanese cucumber, peeled into thin ribbons

1 tablespoon peanut oil

1 teaspoon sesame oil

1 tablespoon fresh coriander leaves

Juice of ½ lime

Sea salt and freshly cracked black pepper to taste

Combine chilli, lime juice and rind, coriander, lime leaves, lemongrass, ginger, onions, fish sauce and sesame oil. Lay each fish on a large piece of aluminium foil, scoop half the chilli and lime mixture inside each fish, then fold the fish up in the foil. Bake on a baking tray at 180°C (350°F) for 20 minutes or until fish is just cooked, serve with juices poured over.

For the salad, combine all ingredients, toss well and serve to the side.

Serves: 2

Total cooking time: 5 minutes preparation, 20 minutes cooking

Coddled eggs and tarragon with grilled prosciutto

Protein

This recipe is great at any time of the day; breakfast, lunch or dinner.

6 prosciutto slices

Eggs

4 eggs, at room temperature

2 teaspoons dried tarragon

1 tablespoon cream

Sea salt and freshly cracked black pepper to taste

For the eggs, break into small individual ramekins, season, sprinkle over tarragon, then pour 1 teaspoon of cream over each. Cover ramekins then place in a saucepan of simmering water; cook over medium heat for 8 minutes. Remove eggs from ramekins and serve on two heated plates. Grill prosciutto and serve with the eggs.

Serves: 2

Total cooking time: 5 minutes preparation, 8 minutes cooking

Lentil and lime soup with onion and coriander

Carbohydrate

If you cannot find French green lentils for this recipe you can substitute them with brown lentils. The brown lentils will take less time to cook so be careful not to overcook them as they quickly lose their shape and turn mushy.

1 onion, sliced

1 garlic clove, crushed

1 teaspoon ground coriander

1 teaspoon ground cumin

1 teaspoon fresh ginger, grated

1 long red chilli, seeded and sliced

½ cup French green lentils

1 tomato, seeded and chopped

4 cups water

Juice of 2 limes

¼ cup coriander leaves

Sea salt and freshly cracked black pepper to taste

Fry onion and garlic with 1 teaspoon of water in a non-stick frying pan until onion softens. Add coriander, cumin, ginger, chilli, lentils, tomatoes and water. Cover and bring to the boil; then reduce heat and allow to simmer for 20 minutes or until lentils are tender. Add lime juice, coriander and seasoning and serve.

Serves: 2

Total cooking time: 5 minutes preparation, 25 minutes cooking

Beef tenderloin with green pepper sauce served with asparagus and bean salad

Protein

Tenderloin steak is cut from the short loin of the animal and is believed to be the most tender cut of all beef steaks. When purchasing steak you should look for a cherry-red hue, and also check that the meat is firm, not mushy, when pressed. This indicates the steak is fresh.

2 beef tenderloin steaks

2 tablespoons olive oil

Green pepper sauce

1 tablespoon olive oil

½ onion, finely chopped

½ cup beef stock

2 teaspoons green peppercorns

2 tablespoons cream

1 tablespoon fresh basil, chopped

Sea salt and freshly cracked black pepper to taste

Asparagus and bean salad

100g (3½ oz) baby beans, trimmed

4 thin green asparagus

Basil almond butter

1 tablespoon butter

1 tablespoon almond slivers

1 tablespoon fresh basil, chopped

Heat oil in a large frying pan and cook steaks for 2–3 minutes each side, or until cooked as preferred. Set steaks aside in a warm place for 10 minutes before serving.

For the green pepper sauce, heat olive oil in the frying pan, then add the onion and cook until lightly brown. Add the stock and peppercorns; bring to the boil then reduce heat and allow to simmer for 5 minutes. Add the cream, gently warm over low heat for 5 minutes. Stir through basil and season.

For the asparagus and bean salad, bring a large saucepan of salted water to the boil, then add the beans and asparagus and cook for 2 minutes or until just tender; drain.

For basil almond butter, melt butter in a saucepan, add the almond slivers and cook for 3 minutes or until golden brown.

Serve steaks with green pepper sauce poured over. Serve asparagus and beans to the side, with almond butter drizzled over and scattered with basil.

Serves: 2
Total cooking time: 5 minutes preparation, 15 minutes cooking

Lamb salad with lemon dressing

Protein

3 lamb fillets

2 tablespoons olive oil

2 spring onions, thinly sliced

1 garlic clove, crushed

1 tablespoon fresh mint, finely chopped

Zest and juice of ½ lemon

Sea salt and freshly cracked black pepper to taste

1 Lebanese cucumber, thinly sliced

½ red onion, thinly sliced

50g (1½ oz) feta cheese, crumbled

4 cups mixed salad leaves

Lemon dressing

1 tablespoon sour cream

1 teaspoon lemon juice

¼ cup olive oil

Combine lamb, oil, spring onion, garlic, mint, zest, juice and seasoning. Allow lamb to marinate for 10 minutes. Cook lamb fillet for 3 minutes each side, baste continuously with the marinade. Allow lamb to rest 5 minutes before slicing thinly. Combine lamb, cucumber, Spanish onion, feta cheese and salad leaves.

For the lemon dressing, combine sour cream, oil and lemon juice; whisk well, then drizzle over the lamb salad. Toss the salad well to combine.

Serves: 2
Total cooking time: 5 minutes preparation, 10 minutes marinating,
11 minutes cooking and resting

Fish fillets with walnut and lemon served with squash and asparagus

Protein

Fish fillets with walnut and lemon

2 tablespoons walnut pieces, finely chopped

Zest of ½ lemon

1 tablespoon fresh flat-leaf parsley, finely chopped

2 large fish fillets

1 tablespoon olive oil

Squash and asparagus stir-fry

1 tablespoon olive oil

2 baby yellow squash, sliced

4 asparagus spears, trimmed

1 tablespoon olive oil, extra

Juice of ½ lemon

1 teaspoon fresh thyme leaves, finely chopped

Sea salt and freshly cracked black pepper to taste

Combine nuts, rind and parsley; set aside. Brush fish with oil then cook on a heated barbecue for 3 minutes each side or until browned and cooked through. Serve fish onto 2 plates and top with walnut and lemon zest mixture.

For the squash and asparagus stir-fry, heat oil in a wok, add squash and asparagus and cook for 5 minutes or until vegetables are tender and cooked through. Combine extra olive oil, lemon juice, thyme and seasoning and drizzle over the vegetables.

Serve fish with vegetables to the side.

Serves: 2

Total cooking time: 5 minutes preparation, 6 minutes cooking

Mixed mushroom omelette

Protein

You can use all sorts of mushrooms for this recipe depending on your budget and taste preference. Use Swiss brown, oyster, field, button, shitake, enoki or portabella mushrooms.

1 tablespoon olive oil

2 tablespoons butter, chopped

200g (7 oz) mixed mushrooms, sliced

1 clove of garlic, finely chopped

2 teaspoons thyme leaves, chopped

1 tablespoon lemon juice

2 tablespoons flat-leaf parsley leaves, chopped

6 eggs, lightly beaten

Sea salt and freshly cracked black pepper to taste

2 tablespoons finely grated Parmesan cheese

Heat olive oil and butter in a large frying pan, add mushrooms and stir-fry 8 minutes or until mushrooms are soft and golden in colour. Add garlic, thyme, lemon juice, parsley and seasoning and cook a further minute. Set aside and keep warm.

Season the beaten eggs. Cook half the egg mixture in a frying pan over medium heat for 5 minutes. Place half the mushroom mixture onto the omelette, sprinkle over 1 tablespoon of the Parmesan cheese, then fold the omelette in half and cook for a further minute before serving onto a plate. Repeat with remaining ingredients.

Serves: 2

Total cooking time: 5 minutes preparation, 20 minutes cooking

Chicken and artichoke skewers served with mixed barbecued vegetables

Protein

Chicken and artichoke skewers

200g (7 oz) diced chicken breast, diced

4 artichoke hearts, halved

8 button mushrooms

½ cup olive oil

Juice of 1 lemon

1 garlic clove, crushed

1 tablespoon dried oregano

Sea salt and freshly cracked black pepper to taste

4 long metal skewers

Mixed barbecued vegetables

1 baby yellow squash, sliced

1 zucchini, sliced lengthways

2 Roma tomatoes, halved

4 asparagus spears, trimmed

Thread chicken pieces, artichoke hearts and mushrooms onto the skewers. Combine all other ingredients together and mix well. Reserve half the marinade, then brush the skewers with the remaining marinade. Barbecue the skewers until browned all over and chicken is cooked through. Baste frequently with the marinade while cooking.

For the mixed barbecued vegetables, cook all vegetables on a heated oiled barbecue for 4–5 minutes each side, baste with reserved marinade as required.

Serves: 2
Total cooking time: 10 minutes preparation, 10 minutes cooking

Chicken burgers with basil and mint served with tomato and feta salad

Protein

Once cooked these burgers are great to freeze for one of those food emergencies when you don't want to cook.

Chicken burgers

250g (8 oz) chicken mince

½ small brown onion, minced

Dash chilli powder, or to taste

1 tablespoon fresh mint leaves, chopped

1 tablespoon fresh basil leaves, chopped

1 egg white, lightly beaten

½ teaspoon sea salt

Dash of pepper

Mixed salad

1 cup mixed salad leaves

50g (1½ oz) feta cheese, crumbled

4 cherry tomatoes, halved

½ Lebanese cucumber, sliced

1 tablespoon lemon juice

1 tablespoon olive oil

Sea salt and freshly cracked black pepper to taste

For the chicken burgers, combine all ingredients. Divide mince mixture into burgers. Cook burgers on a preheated barbecue 3–4 minutes each side or until golden brown and cooked through.

For the mixed salad, combine all ingredients, toss well and serve with the burgers to the side.

Serves: 2

Total cooking time: 15 minutes preparation and cooking

Pork steaks with tomato and tamarind sauce

Protein

Tamarind sauce

1 tablespoon olive oil

½ red onion, finely chopped

3 garlic cloves, crushed

2 Roma tomatoes, seeded and chopped

1 teaspoon tamarind puree

2 fresh long red chillies, seeded and chopped

¼ teaspoon paprika

Pork steaks

2 pork leg steaks

Sea salt and freshly cracked black pepper

2 tablespoons olive oil

2 cups rocket

1 tablespoon olive oil, extra

For the tamarind sauce, heat oil in a frying pan, add onion and garlic and cook until onion is lightly browned. Place onion and garlic in a blender with the tomatoes, tamarind, chilli and paprika; process until smooth.

Baste the pork steaks with half of the tamarind sauce, then season. Heat oil in a frying pan and cook the pork for 2–3 minutes each side or until cooked as desired. Serve pork topped with remaining tamarind sauce. Serve rocket to the side with extra olive oil drizzled over.

Serves: 2
Total cooking time: 5 minutes preparation, 10 minutes cooking

Barbecued lamb cutlets served with rocket salad with feta and walnuts

Protein

Barbecued lamb cutlets

6 trimmed lamb cutlets

2 tablespoons olive oil

Sea salt and freshly cracked black pepper

Rocket salad with feta and walnuts

2 cups rocket

50g (1½ oz) feta cheese, crumbled

2 tablespoons walnut pieces

2 tablespoons olive oil

Baste cutlets with olive oil, then season and cook on a barbecue for 2–3 minutes each side.

For the salad, combine all ingredients and toss well.

Serve cutlets with salad to the side.

Serves: 2

Total cooking time: 5 minutes preparation, 5 minutes cooking

Swordfish with spicy macadamia and mint pesto served with cucumber salad

Protein

Swordfish with spicy macadamia and mint pesto

¼ cup fresh mint leaves

1 tablespoon olive oil

¼ teaspoon dried chilli flakes

8 salted macadamia nuts

1 tablespoon lemon juice

2 swordfish steaks

Cucumber salad

2 Lebanese cucumbers, halved, seeded and finely
   chopped

¼ cup sour cream

2 tablespoons fresh mint, chopped

½ clove garlic, crushed

¼ teaspoon ground cumin

1 teaspoon lemon juice

For the swordfish, combine mint, olive oil, chilli, macadamias and lemon juice in a food processor until well blended. Baste swordfish liberally with half the pesto mixture. Cook fish on oiled barbeque hot plate 1–2 minutes each side or until browned and just cooked through. Serve brushed with the reserved pesto.

For the cucumber salad, combine all ingredients.

Serve swordfish with cucumber salad to the side.

Serves: 2
Total cooking time: 10 minutes preparation, 4 minutes cooking

Sardines wrapped in vine leaves with spiced garlic and almond butter served with fennel, tomato and parsley salad

Protein

Vine leaves are leaves of the grapevine that have been cured. You can buy them preserved in jars in some supermarkets; you should also be readily able to buy them from your local delicatessen. Rinse the vine leaves before use to wash away the excess salt from the brine they are cured in.

Sardines wrapped in vine leaves

2 tablespoons butter

1 garlic clove, crushed

1 teaspoon ground coriander

1 teaspoon ground cumin

2 tablespoons almond slivers

8 large preserved vine leaves

100g (3½ oz) canned sardine fillets in oil

Sea salt and freshly cracked black pepper to taste

1 tablespoon olive oil

Fennel, tomato and parsley salad

¼ cup fennel, finely chopped

1 small tomato, finely chopped

½ cup fresh parsley, finely chopped

1 teaspoon lemon juice

2 tablespoons extra virgin olive oil

Sea salt and freshly cracked black pepper to taste

Melt butter in a frying pan, add garlic, coriander, cumin and almonds; stir-fry 2 minutes over high heat.

Place 2 vine leaves on a flat surface, place a sardine fillet on the vine leaves, top with 2 teaspoons of the garlic and almond butter mixture and season. Wrap sardines up in the vine leaves. Repeat with remaining ingredients.

Heat oil in a large frying pan, cook the wrapped sardines 2 minutes each side.

For the salad, combine all ingredients together.

Serve sardines with salad to the side.

Serves: 2
Total cooking time: 10 minutes preparation, 15 minutes cooking

Stir-fried squid and bok choy

Protein

If you haven't used squid hoods before, you should prepare them as follows. Cut down the length of the hood on one side, open up the hood and with a sharp knife cut a cross hatched pattern on one side of the hood. Slice the squid hood into 5 cm (2 inch) wide pieces lengthways. Don't be timid about using new ingredients as this recipe is very easy to make and very tasty.

2 tablespoons peanut oil

1 teaspoon sesame oil

3 squid hoods, scored and sliced lengthways into
    5 cm (2 inch) wide pieces

1 garlic clove, crushed

¼ teaspoon dried chilli flakes, or to taste

½ teaspoon sea salt

2 spring onions, sliced

3 baby bok choy, quartered lengthways

1 teaspoon fish sauce

2 tablespoons fresh coriander leaves, chopped

Heat oils in a large wok, add squid, garlic, chilli and salt, then stir-fry for 5 minutes or until squid is tender and cooked through. Remove squid from wok and set aside.

Add spring onions, bok choy and fish sauce to the wok, then stir-fry for 5 minutes or until bok choy is tender. Return squid to the wok, briefly stir-fry. Stir through coriander and serve.

Serves: 2

Total cooking time: 5 minutes preparation, 5 minutes cooking

Meal Planning

Using the meal planners
Quick and easy meal planner
Vegetarian meal planner

Using the meal planners

There are two meal planners in this section; a 'quick and easy meal planner' for busy people, and a 'vegetarian meal planner'. The meal planners are both easy to follow and include instructions on preparing food ahead of time for the busy days, as well as shopping lists. The food is all low GI, nutritionally balanced, and follows the *GI Feel Good* formula.

The plans are both designed for two people, so the shopping lists include food for two people for one week. You should try to prepare food in advance as much as possible so that less time is required for food preparation throughout your day. Suggestions for the food that you can prepare ahead are also included.

Both the meal plans are designed for healthy adults. Children, teenagers, pregnant or breastfeeding women and people with illnesses have different nutritional requirements and should consult their dietician or health professional. You should consult your health professional before beginning any dietary plan.

Quick and easy meal planner

The 'quick and easy meal planner' is designed for busy people. The amount of food preparation is kept to a minimum, for those who don't have time to spend in the kitchen. The types of ingredients used should be easily found in your local supermarket so there is no need to spend extra time searching for specialised ingredients at various stores. The variety in the menu has also been minimised to avoid excessive cooking requirements. It is assumed that you will be quite happy to each muesli five days of the week if it saves time.

The meal planner is designed around a five-day working week with the sixth and seventh day of each week designated as non-working days. It is assumed that you will have more time for food preparation on these days and the meals are planned accordingly. Remember that the shopping list is designed for two people. If you are shopping for one, halve the ingredients.

Week 1 shopping

Vegetables

6 tomatoes
11 Roma tomatoes
20 grape tomatoes
1 avocado
30 button mushrooms
200g (7 oz) mixed
  mushrooms
2 red onions
1 brown onion
2 white onions
¼ fennel bulb
100g (3½ oz) green
  beans
½ broccoli head
1 baby yellow squash
2 green zucchini
½ yellow zucchini
4 Lebanese
  eggplants
1 bunch broccolini
½ red capsicum
7 celery sticks
½ red birds-eye chilli
½ long red chilli
6 garlic cloves
4 cups rocket leaves
1 baby cos lettuce
2 cups parsley
1 tblsp coriander
1 tblsp mint
1 tblsp oregano
20 basil leaves
4 rosemary stems
2 tsp thyme

Fruit

1 mandarin
2½ lemons
½ lime
6 x 140g (4½ oz)
  punnets diced
  peaches in natural
  juice

2 x 140g (4½ oz)
  punnets diced
  apricots in natural
  juice
2 x 140g (4½ oz)
  punnets diced pears
  in natural juice

Meat and seafood

100g (3½ oz) smoked
  salmon
2 beef medallions
2 white fish fillets
1 chicken breast
10 slices prosciutto
2 lamb backstrap
2 kg (4 lbs) chicken
  bones
250g (9 oz) beef

Dairy case

700g (23 oz) ricotta
8 tblsp butter
1¼ cups Parmesan
  cheese
1¼ cups grated
  cheese
6 tblsp cream
100g (3½ oz)
  bocconcini
200g (7 oz) haloumi
4 serves of cheese

Grocery

700g (23 oz) rolled
  oats
100g (3½ oz)
  processed bran
60g (2 oz) coarse
  oatmeal
200g (7 oz) dried
  apricots
26 eggs
Sea salt

Black pepper
400ml (1½ cups) olive
  oil
1 tblsp walnuts
1 tblsp baby salted
  capers
½ tblsp tomato paste
7 canned anchovies
50ml (1½ fl oz) white
  wine vinegar
1 tblsp red wine
  vinegar
400g (14 oz) canned
  diced tomatoes
1 vanilla bean pod
½ tsp chilli powder
1½ tblsp dried
  oregano
2½ tblsp dried
  thyme
2 tsp paprika
¼ tsp nutmeg
2 tsp tarragon
1 tblsp mixed dried
  herbs
3 bay leaves
10 whole black
  peppercorn
250g (8 oz) frozen
  spinach
Decaffeinated tea
Camomile tea
Peppermint tea
Lemon tea
3 litres (3 cups)
  malt-free soymilk

NB: Substitute fresh herbs with dried herbs, if desired, where
  appropriate.

Week 1 preparation and cooking

Muesli with apricots, mandarin and vanilla: This recipe will make enough for 5 bowls of muesli each. Keep your muesli in an airtight container.

Smoked salmon dip: This recipe will make enough dip for 5 servings each with the *Vegetable crudités*.

Baked ricotta tarts with roast tomatoes and basil: This recipe makes enough for 2 people for 2 lunches each; 3 ricotta tarts per person per meal. Keep the ricotta tarts refrigerated.

Spinach roulade with mushroom and cheese filling: This recipe makes enough for 2 people for 2 servings each. Keep refrigerated.

Chicken stock: This will be used in the *Tomato and fennel soup* on day 6. Use the required amount of stock for the soup then freeze the remainder.

Day 1

Breakfast (Carbohydrate)

- *Muesli with apricots, mandarin and vanilla.* Serve with malt-free soymilk and top with diced peaches in natural juice
- Beverage suggestion – 1 cup of decaffeinated, or 97% caffeine-free, tea with optional malt-free soymilk

Wait at least three hours after breakfast before lunch

Lunch (Protein)

- *Egg roll-ups*
- Beverage suggestion – 1 cup of peppermint tea
- Beverage suggestion – 1 glass of water

Snack (Protein)

- *Vegetable crudités* served with *Smoked salmon dip*
- Beverage suggestion – 1 glass of water

Dinner (Protein)

- *Beef medallions with zucchini, caper and lemon salad*
- Beverage suggestion – 1 cup of lemon herbal tea
- Beverage suggestion – 1 glass of water

Day 2

Breakfast (Carbohydrate)

- *Muesli with apricots, mandarin and vanilla.* Serve with malt-free soymilk and top with diced apricots in natural juice
- Beverage suggestion – 1 cup of decaffeinated, or 97% caffeine-free, tea with optional malt-free soymilk

Wait at least three hours after breakfast before lunch

Lunch (Protein)

- *Baked ricotta tarts with roast tomatoes and basil*
- Beverage suggestion – 1 cup of peppermint tea
- Beverage suggestion – 1 glass of water

Snack (Protein)

- *Vegetable crudités* served with *Smoked salmon dip*
- Beverage suggestion – 1 glass of water

Dinner (Protein)

- *Spicy fish fillets with tomato salsa served with garlic and chilli broccolini*
- Beverage suggestion – 1 cup of camomile tea
- Beverage suggestion – 1 glass of water

Day 3

Breakfast (Carbohydrate)

- *Muesli with apricots, mandarin and vanilla.* Serve with malt-free soymilk and top with diced peaches in natural juice
- Beverage suggestion – 1 cup of decaffeinated, or 97% caffeine-free, tea with optional malt-free soymilk

Wait at least three hours after breakfast before lunch

Lunch (Protein)

- *Spinach roulade with mushroom and cheese filling*
- Beverage suggestion – 1 cup of peppermint tea
- Beverage suggestion – 1 glass of water

Snack (Protein)

- *Vegetable crudités* served with *Smoked salmon dip*
- Beverage suggestion – 1 glass of water

Dinner (Protein)

- *Chicken Caesar salad*
- Beverage suggestion – 1 cup of camomile tea
- Beverage suggestion – 1 glass of water

Day 4

Breakfast (Carbohydrate)

- *Muesli with apricots, mandarin and vanilla.* Serve with malt-free soymilk and top with diced pears in natural juice
- Beverage suggestion – 1 cup of decaffeinated, or 97% caffeine-free, tea with optional malt-free soymilk

Wait at least three hours after breakfast before lunch

Lunch (Protein)

- *Baked ricotta tarts with roast tomatoes and basil*
- Beverage suggestion – 1 cup of peppermint tea
- Beverage suggestion – 1 glass of water

Snack (Protein)

- *Vegetable crudités* served with *Smoked salmon dip*
- Beverage suggestion – 1 glass of water

Dinner (Protein)

- *Vegetable kebabs with Cajun spices and tomato salsa*
- Beverage suggestion – 1 cup of lemon herbal tea
- Beverage suggestion – 1 glass of water

Day 5

Breakfast (Carbohydrate)

- *Muesli with apricots, mandarin and vanilla.* Serve with malt-free soymilk and top with diced peaches in natural juice
- Beverage suggestion – 1 cup of decaffeinated, or 97% caffeine-free, tea with optional malt-free soymilk

Wait at least three hours after breakfast before lunch

Lunch (Protein)

- *Spinach roulade with mushroom and cheese filling*
- Beverage suggestion – 1 cup of peppermint tea
- Beverage suggestion – 1 glass of water

Snack (Protein)

- *Vegetable crudités* served with *Smoked salmon dip*
- Beverage suggestion – 1 glass of water

Dinner (Protein)

- *Lamb with thyme and garlic served with fresh tomato and bocconcini salad*
- Beverage suggestion – 1 cup of peppermint tea
- Beverage suggestion – 1 glass of water

Day 6

Breakfast (Protein)

- *Coddled eggs and tarragon with grilled prosciutto*
- Beverage suggestion – 1 cup of peppermint tea
- Beverage suggestion – 1 glass of water

Lunch (Protein)

- *Tomato and fennel soup*
- Beverage suggestion – 1 glass of water

Snack (Protein)

- One serve of cheese
- Beverage suggestion – 1 glass of water

Dinner (Protein)

- *Roast chicken served with steamed vegetables with butter and thyme*
- Beverage suggestion – 1 cup of camomile tea
- Beverage suggestion – 1 glass of water

Day 7

Breakfast (Protein)

- *Mixed mushroom omelette*
- Beverage suggestion – 1 cup of camomile tea
- Beverage suggestion – 1 glass of water

Lunch (Protein)

- *Grilled haloumi, tomato and eggplant salad*
- Beverage suggestion – 1 cup of peppermint tea
- Beverage suggestion – 1 glass of water

Snack (Protein)

- One serve of cheese
- Beverage suggestion – 1 glass of water

Dinner (Protein)

- *Beef stir-fry with green beans and broccoli*
- Beverage suggestion – 1 cup of peppermint tea
- Beverage suggestion – 1 glass of water

Week 2 shopping

Vegetables

1 green capsicum
1 red capsicum
7 tomatoes
200g (7 oz) grape tomatoes
2 Roma tomatoes
16 button mushrooms
2 oyster mushrooms
3 shitake mushrooms
3 Swiss brown mushrooms
2 flat mushrooms
2 zucchini
2 yellow squash
4 asparagus spears
1 cucumber
1½ cups wom bok
½ broccoli head
200g (7 oz) green beans
1½ eggplants
½ fennel bulb
1 Lebanese cucumber
2 celery sticks
1 red onion
6 spring onions
1 brown onion
4 garlic cloves
1½ long red chillies
¼ cup alfalfa
2 slices ginger
6 cups rocket leaves
50g (1½ oz) baby spinach leaves
2 tblsp basil
3 tsp thyme
½ cup parsley
½ tblsp mint
½ cup coriander
2 tblsp Vietnamese mint
1 tblsp oregano
½ cup Thai basil
2 tsp chives
2 tsp dill

Fruit

2 lemons
2 serves of fruit
4 x 140g (4½ oz) punnet diced peaches in natural juice
4 x 140g (4½ oz) punnet diced pears in natural juice
2 x 140g (4½ oz) punnet diced apricots in natural juice

Meat and seafood

4 chicken breasts
200g (7 oz) large cooked prawns
240g (7½ oz) pork
250g (9 oz) beef mince
2 large fish fillets
6 slices pancetta
6 lamb cutlets
50g (1½ oz) smoked salmon
2 bacon rashers
2 sirloin steaks

Dairy case

400g (14 oz) ricotta
½ cup Parmesan cheese
8 serves cheese
5 tblsp butter
¾ cup cream
75g (2½ oz) blue vein cheese
1 tblsp sour cream

Groceries

700g (23 oz) rolled oats
100g (3½ oz) processed bran
60g (2 oz) coarse oatmeal
200g (7 oz) diced apricots
3 litres (3 cups) soymilk
Decaffeinated tea
Camomile tea
Peppermint tea
Lemon tea
1 cup basmati rice
420g (15 oz) canned kidney beans
400g (14 oz) canned chickpeas
25g (1 oz) sun-dried tomatoes
250g (9 oz) frozen spinach
14 eggs
2 canned anchovies
300ml (1¼ cups) olive oil
1 tblsp vegetable oil
3 tblsp peanut oil
1 tsp sesame oil
1 tblsp white wine vinegar
4 slices Performax or low GI bread
2 tblsp walnut pieces
1 tsp Cajun spice
½ tsp chilli powder
½ tblsp red wine vinegar
Dash cayenne pepper
¼ tsp paprika
¼ tsp shrimp paste
½ tsp dried chilli flakes
1 tblsp fish sauce
¼ tsp nutmeg
½ tsp cumin
½ tsp ground coriander
1 tblsp dried oregano

1 tsp tarragon		
⅛ tsp mustard powder		
1 star anise		
2 cloves		
½ cinnamon stick		
Sea salt		
Black pepper		

NB: Substitute fresh herbs with dried herbs, if desired, where appropriate.

Week 2 preparation and cooking

Muesli with apricots, mandarin and vanilla: This recipe will make enough for 5 bowls of muesli each. Keep your muesli in an airtight container.

Cajun spiced basmati rice salad with tomatoes, red kidney beans and fresh herbs: This recipe makes enough for 2 people for 2 lunches each. Keep refrigerated until ready for use.

Chickpea dip: Halve this recipe for 2 serves each with vegetable crudités.

Spinach and Parmesan cheese bake with ricotta and blue vein cheese: This recipe makes enough for 2 people for 2 serve each.

Day 8

Breakfast (Carbohydrate)

- *Muesli with apricots, mandarin and vanilla*. Serve with malt-free soymilk and top with diced pears in natural juice
- Beverage suggestion – 1 cup of decaffeinated, or 97% caffeine-free, tea with optional malt-free soymilk

Lunch (Carbohydrate)

- *Cajun spiced basmati rice salad with tomatoes, red kidney beans and fresh herbs*
- Beverage suggestion – 1 cup of decaffeinated, or 97% caffeine-free, tea with optional malt-free soymilk
- Beverage suggestion – 1 glass of water

Snack (Carbohydrate)

- *Vegetable crudités* with *Chickpea dip*
- Beverage suggestion – 1 glass of water

Wait at least three hours after your snack before eating dinner

Dinner (Protein)

- *Chicken breast stuffed with ricotta and sun-dried tomatoes, served with chilli tomato sauce and rocket salad*
- Beverage suggestion – 1 cup of peppermint tea
- Beverage suggestion – 1 glass of water

Day 9

Breakfast (Carbohydrate)

- *Muesli with apricots, mandarin and vanilla.* Serve with malt-free soymilk and top with diced peaches in natural juice
- Beverage suggestion – 1 cup of decaffeinated, or 97% caffeine-free, tea with optional malt-free soymilk

Wait at least three hours after breakfast before eating lunch

Lunch (Protein)

- *Asian prawn salad with chilli and lime dressing*
- Beverage suggestion – 1 cup of peppermint tea
- Beverage suggestion – 1 glass of water

Snack (Protein)

- One serve of cheese
- Beverage suggestion – 1 glass of water

Dinner (Protein)

- *Vegetable stir-fry*
- Beverage suggestion – 1 cup of camomile tea
- Beverage suggestion – 1 glass of water

Day 10

Breakfast (Carbohydrate)

- *Muesli with apricots, mandarin and vanilla*. Serve with malt-free soymilk and top with diced apricots in natural juice
- Beverage suggestion – 1 cup of decaffeinated, or 97% caffeine-free, tea with optional malt-free soymilk

Lunch (Carbohydrate)

- *Cajun spiced basmati rice salad with tomatoes, red kidney beans and fresh herbs*
- Beverage suggestion – 1 cup of decaffeinated, or 97% caffeine-free, tea with optional malt-free soymilk
- Beverage suggestion – 1 glass of water

Snack (Carbohydrate)

- *Vegetable crudités* with *Chickpea dip*
- Beverage suggestion – 1 glass of water

Wait at least three hours after your snack before eating dinner

Dinner (Protein)

- *Pork and eggplant stir-fry*
- Beverage suggestion – 1 cup of camomile tea
- Beverage suggestion – 1 glass of water

Day 11

Breakfast (Carbohydrate)

- *Muesli with apricots, mandarin and vanilla.* Serve with malt-free soymilk and top with diced peaches in natural juice
- Beverage suggestion – 1 cup of decaffeinated, or 97% caffeine-free, tea with optional malt-free soymilk

Wait at least three hours after breakfast before eating lunch

Lunch (Protein)

- *Spinach and Parmesan cheese bake with ricotta and blue vein cheese*
- Beverage suggestion – 1 cup of peppermint tea
- Beverage suggestion – 1 glass of water

Snack (Protein)

- One serve of cheese
- Beverage suggestion – 1 glass of water

Dinner (Protein)

- *Shish-kebabs with tomato and baby spinach leaf salad*
- Beverage suggestion – 1 cup of camomile tea
- Beverage suggestion – 1 glass of water

Day 12

Breakfast (Carbohydrate)

- *Muesli with apricots, mandarin and vanilla.* Serve with malt-free soymilk and top with diced pears in natural juice
- Beverage suggestion – 1 cup of decaffeinated, or 97% caffeine-free, tea with optional malt-free soymilk

Lunch (Carbohydrate)

- *Performax sandwiches with oregano and mustard vinaigrette*
- Beverage suggestion - 1 cup of decaffeinated, or 97% caffeine-free, tea with optional malt-free soymilk
- Beverage suggestion – 1 glass of water

Snack (Carbohydrate)

- One serve of fruit
- Beverage suggestion – 1 glass of water

Wait at least three hours after your snack before eating dinner

Dinner (Protein)

- *Fish fillets with walnut and lemon served with squash and asparagus*
- Beverage suggestion – 1 cup of camomile tea
- Beverage suggestion – 1 glass of water

Day 13

Breakfast (Protein)

- *Scrambled eggs with garlic mushrooms and grilled pancetta*
- Beverage suggestion – 1 cup of lemon tea
- Beverage suggestion – 1 glass of water

Lunch (Protein)

- *Spinach and Parmesan cheese bake with ricotta and blue vein cheese*
- Beverage suggestion – 1 cup of peppermint tea
- Beverage suggestion – 1 glass of water

Snack (Protein)

- One serve of cheese
- Beverage suggestion – 1 glass of water

Dinner (Protein)

- *Lamb cutlets with grilled zucchini and tomato salad*
- Beverage suggestion – 1 cup of peppermint tea
- Beverage suggestion – 1 glass of water

Day 14

Breakfast (Protein)

- *Zucchini and smoked salmon frittata with snipped chives and fresh dill*
- Beverage suggestion – 1 cup of lemon tea
- Beverage suggestion – 1 glass of water

Lunch (Protein)

- *Creamy Asian chicken soup*
- Beverage suggestion – 1 cup of camomile tea

Snack (Protein)

- One serve of cheese
- Beverage suggestion – 1 glass of water

Dinner (Protein)

- *Steak with mushrooms, spring onions and anchovy and tarragon butter*
- Beverage suggestion – 1 cup of camomile tea
- Beverage suggestion – 1 glass of water

Week 3 shopping

Vegetables
1 fennel bulb
7 celery sticks
4 cherry tomatoes
12 grape tomatoes
3 tomatoes
5 yellow squash
3 zucchini
100g (3½ oz) green beans
20 asparagus
1 eggplant
¼ red capsicum
¼ yellow capsicum
½ avocado
12 button mushrooms
1 Lebanese cucumber
½ cucumber
3 baby bok choy
¼ cup alfalfa
2 red onions
2 white onions
10 spring onions
3 brown onions
6 garlic cloves
3 cups rocket leaves
1 cup baby Spinach leaves
1 cup mixed salad leaves
½ long red chilli
½ birds-eye chilli
2 tblsp oregano
1½ cups parsley
4 tblsp mint
¾ cup basil
3 tblsp coriander
1½ tblsp chives
3 rosemary stems
½ cup dill

Fruit
4 lemons
6 serves of fruit
¼ lime
4 x 140g (4½ oz) punnet of diced pears in natural juice
4 x 140g (4½ oz) punnet of diced peaches in natural juice
2 x 140g (4½ oz) punnet of diced apricots in natural juice

Meat and seafood
250g (8 oz) chicken mince
4 bacon rashers
150g (5 oz) smoked salmon
3 squid hoods
250g (8 oz) beef
1 chicken breast
6 slices prosciutto
300g (9½ oz) fish fillets
1 kg (2 lbs) fish bones
300g (9½ oz) diced lamb
2 salmon steaks

Dairy case
50g (1½ oz) feta
2 tblsp butter
700g (23 oz) ricotta
¾ cup mozzarella
¼ cup Parmesan cheese
2 tblsp cream
2½ tblsp sour cream
2 triangles kefalograviera
2 serves of cheese

Grocery
700g (23 oz) rolled oats
100g (3½ oz) processed bran
60g (2 oz) coarse oatmeal
200g (7 oz) dried apricots
3 litres (8 cups) malt-free soymilk
Decaffeinated tea
Camomile tea
Peppermint tea
Lemon tea
2 cups basmati rice
400g (14 oz) canned artichoke hearts
4 tblsp white wine vinegar
3½ bay leaves
10 black peppercorns
Dash chilli powder
22 eggs
250 ml (1 cup) olive oil
2 tblsp peanut oil
1 tsp sesame oil
¼ tsp dried chilli flakes
1 tsp fish sauce
1 tsp mixed dried herbs
1 clove
200g (14 oz) canned diced tomatoes
½ tblsp tomato paste
4 slices Performax or low GI bread
½ tsp oregano
¼ tsp mustard powder
2 tsp tarragon
1 tsp turmeric
1 tsp coriander
½ tblsp curry powder
Sea salt
Black pepper

NB: Substitute fresh herbs with dried herbs, if desired, where appropriate.

Week 3 preparation and cooking

Risotto with artichoke and fennel: This recipe makes enough for 2 people for 2 servings each.

Vegetable stock: Use the required amount of vegetable stock for *Risotto with artichoke and fennel* then freeze the remainder.

Egg and bacon pies: Makes enough pies for 2 people for 2 serves each; 2 pies per serving.

Smoked salmon dip: Makes enough for 2 people for 3 snacks each with *Vegetable crudités*.

Fish stock: Use the required amount of fish stock for *Creamy fish soup with fresh chives*, then freeze the remainder.

Day 15

Breakfast (Carbohydrate)

- *Muesli with apricots, mandarin and vanilla.* Serve with malt-free soymilk and top with diced peaches in natural juice
- Beverage suggestion – 1 cup of decaffeinated, or 97% caffeine-free, tea with optional malt-free soymilk

Lunch (Carbohydrate)

- *Risotto with artichoke and fennel*
- Beverage suggestion – 1 cup of decaffeinated, or 97% caffeine-free, tea with optional malt-free soymilk
- Beverage suggestion – 1 glass of water

Snack (Carbohydrate)

- Serve of fruit
- Beverage suggestion – 1 glass of water

Wait at least three hours after your snack before eating dinner

Dinner (Protein)

- *Chicken burgers with basil and mint served with tomato and feta salad*
- Beverage suggestion – 1 cup of lemon tea
- Beverage suggestion – 1 glass of water

Day 16

Breakfast (Carbohydrate)

- *Muesli with apricots, mandarin and vanilla.* Serve with malt-free soymilk and top with diced pears in natural juice
- Beverage suggestion – 1 cup of decaffeinated, or 97% caffeine-free, tea with optional malt-free soymilk

Wait at least three hours after breakfast before eating lunch

Lunch (Protein)

- *Egg and bacon pies*
- Beverage suggestion – 1 cup of peppermint tea
- Beverage suggestion – 1 glass of water

Snack (Protein)

- *Vegetable crudités* with *Smoked salmon dip*
- Beverage suggestion – 1 glass of water

Dinner (Protein)

- *Avocado and tomato salsa with barbecued vegetables*
- Beverage suggestion – 1 cup of camomile tea
- Beverage suggestion – 1 glass of water

Day 17

Breakfast (Carbohydrate)

- *Muesli with apricots, mandarin and vanilla.* Serve with malt-free soymilk and top with diced peaches in natural juice
- Beverage suggestion – 1 cup of decaffeinated, or 97% caffeine-free, tea with optional malt-free soymilk

Lunch (Carbohydrate)

- *Risotto with artichoke and fennel*
- Beverage suggestion – 1 cup of decaffeinated, or 97% caffeine-free, tea with optional malt-free soymilk
- Beverage suggestion – 1 glass of water

Snack (Carbohydrate)

- One serve of fruit
- Beverage suggestion – 1 glass of water

Wait at least three hours after your snack before eating dinner

Dinner (Protein)

- *Stir-fried squid and bok choy*
- Beverage suggestion – 1 cup of camomile tea
- Beverage suggestion – 1 glass of water

Day 18

Breakfast (Carbohydrate)

- *Muesli with apricots, mandarin and vanilla*. Serve with malt-free soymilk and top with diced apricots in natural juice
- Beverage suggestion – 1 cup of decaffeinated, or 97% caffeine-free, tea with optional malt-free soymilk

Wait at least three hours after breakfast before eating lunch

Lunch (Protein)

- *Egg and bacon pies*
- Beverage suggestion – 1 cup of peppermint tea
- Beverage suggestion – 1 glass of water

Snack (Protein)

- *Vegetable crudités* with *Smoked salmon dip*
- Beverage suggestion – 1 glass of water

Dinner (Protein)

- *Beef burgers with tomato sauce, served with minted asparagus and squash*
- Beverage suggestion – 1 cup of lemon tea
- Beverage suggestion – 1 glass of water

Day 19

Breakfast (Carbohydrate)

- *Muesli with apricots, mandarin and vanilla.* Serve with malt-free soymilk and top with diced pears in natural juice
- Beverage suggestion – 1 cup of decaffeinated, or 97% caffeine-free, tea with optional malt-free soymilk

Lunch (Carbohydrate)

- *Performax sandwiches with oregano and mustard vinaigrette*
- Beverage suggestion – 1 cup of decaffeinated, or 97% caffeine-free, tea with optional malt-free soymilk
- Beverage suggestion – 1 glass of water

Snack (Carbohydrate)

- One serve of fruit
- Beverage suggestion – 1 glass of water

Wait at least three hours after your snack before eating dinner

Dinner (Protein)

- *Egg crepes with chicken, tomato and spinach, drizzled with garlic mayonnaise*
- Beverage suggestion – 1 cup of peppermint tea
- Beverage suggestion – 1 glass of water

Day 20

Breakfast (Protein)

- *Coddled eggs and tarragon with grilled prosciutto*
- Beverage suggestion – 1 cup of peppermint tea
- Beverage suggestion – 1 glass of water

Lunch (Protein)

- *Creamy fish soup with fresh chives*
- Beverage suggestion – 1 glass of water

Snack (Protein)

- One serve of cheese
- Beverage suggestion – 1 glass of water

Dinner (Protein)

- *Lamb curry*
- Beverage suggestion – 1 cup of camomile tea
- Beverage suggestion – 1 glass of water

Day 21

Breakfast (Protein)

- *Omelette with salmon, sour cream and fresh herbs*
- Beverage suggestion – 1 cup of peppermint tea
- Beverage suggestion – 1 glass of water

Lunch (Protein)

- *Saganaki served with rocket*
- Beverage suggestion – 1 glass of water

Snack (Protein)

- *Vegetable crudités* with *Salmon dip*
- Beverage suggestion – 1 glass of water

Dinner (Protein)

- *Salmon steaks served on asparagus with fresh dill dressing*
- Beverage suggestion – 1 cup of camomile tea
- Beverage suggestion – 1 glass of water

Vegetarian meal planner

The vegetarian meal planner is designed for vegetarians who will eat eggs, cream, cheese and fish. If your vegetarian diet is more restrictive you will find plenty of recipes in this book and on our website that you can substitute for the foods you are unable to eat.

The recipes and ingredients used in this meal planner focus on making things quick and easy for you. All the ingredients should be easily found in your local supermarket so there is no need to spend extra time searching for specialised ingredients at various stores. The variety in the menu has also been minimised to avoid excessive cooking requirements. It is assumed that you will be quite happy to each muesli five days of the week if it saves time.

The meal planner is designed around a five-day working week with the sixth and seventh day of each week designated as non-working days. It is assumed that you will have more time for food preparation on these days and the meals are planned accordingly. Remember that the shopping list is designed for two people. If you are shopping for one, halve the ingredients.

Week 1 shopping

Vegetables	Fruit	Grocery
6 tomatoes	2 lemons	700g (23 oz) rolled
16 grape tomatoes	1 lime	oats
4 avocado	4 x 140g (4½ oz)	100g (3½ oz)
6 celery sticks	punnet diced	processed bran
24 button mushrooms	peaches in natural	60g (2 oz) coarse
200g (7 oz) green	juice	oatmeal
beans	4 x 140g (4½ oz)	200g (7 oz) dried
2 broccoli heads	punnet diced pears	apricots
1 cauliflower head	in natural juice	3 litres (8 cups) malt-
4 asparagus spears	2 x 140g (4½ oz)	free soymilk
2 baby bok choy	punnet diced	Decaffeinated tea
3 oyster mushrooms	apricots in natural	Camomile tea
100g (3½ oz) mixed	juice	Peppermint tea
mushrooms		Lemon tea
1 red capsicum	**Dairy case**	16 eggs
1 yellow capsicum	6 serves of cheese	Sea salt
10 sun-dried	1 kg (2 lb) ricotta	Black pepper
tomatoes	5 tblsp butter	350ml (1¼ cups) olive
2 Lebanese eggplants	¾ cup cream	oil
2 Roma tomatoes	100g (3½ oz) Gruyere	2 tblsp peanut oil
6 zucchini	cheese	1 tsp sesame oil
3 baby yellow squash	200g (7 oz) haloumi	3 tblsp almond
1 fennel	cheese	slivers
½ eggplant	2 tblsp Parmesan	½ tsp oregano
1 cup baby spinach	cheese	½ tsp paprika
leaves	100g (3½ oz) feta	3 bay leaves
6 large radicchio	2 triangles kefalo-	10 peppercorns
leaves	graviera	1 tblsp red wine
6 cups rocket leaves	1½ tblsp sour cream	vinegar
2 red onions		2 tsp baby capers
10 spring onions		2 tblsp vegetable oil
2 white onions		2 tsp fenugreek seeds
2½ brown onions		1 tsp chilli powder
6 garlic cloves		2 tsp curry powder
4 long green chillies		800g (28 oz) canned
½ birds-eye chilli		diced tomatoes
1 tsp ginger		2 tsp ground
3 tblsp coriander		coriander
1 tblsp Thai basil		1 tsp cumin
2 cups parsley		8 preserved vine
4 rosemary stems		leaves
1 tblsp basil		100g (3½ oz) sardine
1½ tblsp oregano		fillets in oil
1 tsp thyme		350g (12 oz) canned
1 tblsp mint		asparagus spears

NB: Substitute fresh herbs with dried herbs, if desired, where appropriate.

Week 1 preparation and cooking

Guacamole dip: This recipe makes enough dip for 2 people for 3 serves of guacamole with *Vegetable crudités*.

Baked ricotta with capsicum, sun-dried tomatoes and parsley: This recipe makes enough for 2 people for 2 servings each.

Cauliflower and broccoli soup with Gruyere cheese: This recipe make enough soup for 2 people for 2 servings each.

Vegetable stock: Use this stock for the *Cauliflower and broccoli soup with Gruyere cheese* and also for *Asparagus soup*. Freeze any remaining stock.

Zucchini and tomato curry with coriander and fenugreek: This recipe makes enough for 2 people for 2 servings each.

Day 1

Breakfast (Carbohydrate)

- *Muesli with apricots, mandarin and vanilla.* Serve with malt-free soymilk and top with diced peaches in natural juice
- Beverage suggestion – 1 cup of decaffeinated, or 97% caffeine-free, tea with optional malt-free soymilk

Wait at least three hours after breakfast before eating lunch

Lunch (Protein)

- *Egg roll-ups*
- Beverage suggestion – 1 cup of peppermint tea
- Beverage suggestion – 1 glass of water

Snack (Protein)

- *Vegetable crudités* with *Guacamole dip*
- Beverage suggestion – 1 glass of water

Dinner (Protein)

- *Asian-style braised vegetables*
- Beverage suggestion – 1 cup of lemon tea
- Beverage suggestion – 1 glass of water

Day 2

Breakfast (Carbohydrate)

- *Muesli with apricots, mandarin and vanilla.* Serve with malt-free soymilk and top with diced pears in natural juice
- Beverage suggestion – 1 cup of decaffeinated, or 97% caffeine-free, tea with optional malt-free soymilk

Wait at least three hours after breakfast before eating lunch

Lunch (Protein)

- *Baked ricotta with capsicum, sun-dried tomatoes and parsley*
- Beverage suggestion – 1 cup of peppermint tea
- Beverage suggestion – 1 glass of water

Snack (Protein)

- *Vegetable crudités* with *Guacamole dip*
- Beverage suggestion – 1 glass of water

Dinner (Protein)

- *Scrambled eggs with tomato and mushroom*
- Beverage suggestion – 1 cup of camomile tea
- Beverage suggestion – 1 glass of water

Day 3

Breakfast (Carbohydrate)

- *Muesli with apricots, mandarin and vanilla.* Serve with malt-free soymilk and top with diced apricots in natural juice
- Beverage suggestion – 1 cup of decaffeinated, or 97% caffeine-free, tea with optional malt-free soymilk

Wait at least three hours after breakfast before eating lunch

Lunch (Protein)

- *Cauliflower and broccoli soup with Gruyere cheese*
- Beverage suggestion – 1 cup of peppermint tea
- Beverage suggestion – 1 glass of water

Snack (Protein)

- Mixed cheese platter
- Beverage suggestion – 1 glass of water

Dinner (Protein)

- *Grilled haloumi, tomato and eggplant salad*
- Beverage suggestion – 1 cup of lemon tea
- Beverage suggestion – 1 glass of water

Day 4

Breakfast (Carbohydrate)

- *Muesli with apricots, mandarin and vanilla.* Serve with malt-free soymilk and top with diced peaches in natural juice
- Beverage suggestion – 1 cup of decaffeinated, or 97% caffeine-free, tea with optional malt-free soymilk

Wait at least three hours after breakfast before eating lunch

Lunch (Protein)

- *Baked ricotta with capsicum, sun-dried tomatoes and parsley*
- Beverage suggestion – 1 cup of peppermint tea
- Beverage suggestion – 1 glass of water

Snack (Protein)

- *Vegetables crudités* with *Guacamole dip*
- Beverage suggestion – 1 glass of water

Dinner (Protein)

- *Zucchini and tomato curry with coriander and fenugreek*
- Beverage suggestion – 1 cup of peppermint tea
- Beverage suggestion – 1 glass of water

Day 5

Breakfast (Carbohydrate)

- *Muesli with apricots, mandarin and vanilla.* Serve with malt-free soymilk and top with diced pears in natural juice
- Beverage suggestion – 1 cup of decaffeinated, or 97% caffeine-free, tea with optional malt-free soymilk

Wait at least three hours after breakfast before eating lunch

Lunch (Protein)

- *Cauliflower and broccoli soup with Gruyere cheese*
- Beverage suggestion – 1 cup of peppermint tea
- Beverage suggestion – 1 glass of water

Snack (Protein)

- Mixed cheese platter
- Beverage suggestion – 1 glass of water

Dinner (Protein)

- *Vegetable stir-fry*
- Beverage suggestion – 1 cup of camomile tea
- Beverage suggestion – 1 glass of water

Day 6

Breakfast (Protein)

- *Mixed mushroom omelette*
- Beverage suggestion – 1 cup of camomile tea

Lunch (Protein)

- *Radicchio and feta rolls*
- Beverage suggestion – 1 cup of peppermint tea
- Beverage suggestion – 1 glass of water

Snack (Protein)

- *Vegetable crudités*
- Beverage suggestion – 1 glass of water

Dinner (Protein)

- *Sardines wrapped in vine leaves with spiced garlic and almond butter served with fennel, tomato and parsley salad*
- Beverage suggestion – 1 cup of lemon tea
- Beverage suggestion – 1 glass of water

Day 7

Breakfast (Protein)

- *Saganaki served with rocket*
- Beverage suggestion – 1 cup of peppermint tea

Lunch (Protein)

- *Asparagus soup*
- Beverage suggestion – 1 cup of peppermint tea
- Beverage suggestion – 1 glass of water

Snack (Protein)

- Mixed cheese platter
- Beverage suggestion – 1 glass of water

Dinner (Protein)

- *Zucchini and tomato curry with coriander and fenugreek*
- Beverage suggestion – 1 cup of camomile tea
- Beverage suggestion – 1 glass of water

Week 2 shopping

Vegetables	Fruit	Grocery
1 leek	4 x 140g (4½ oz)	700g (23 oz) rolled
6 zucchini	punnet diced	oats
½ cup peas	peaches in natural	100g (3½ oz)
4 baby yellow squash	juice	processed bran
100g (3½ oz) green	4 x 140g (4½ oz)	60g (2 oz) coarse
beans	punnet diced pears	oatmeal
1 head broccoli	in natural juice	200g (7 oz) dried
3 Roma tomatoes	2 x 140g (4½ oz)	apricots
5 tomatoes	punnet diced	3 litres (8 cups)
12 grape tomatoes	apricots in natural	soymilk
22 button mushrooms	juice	Decaffeinated tea
1 Lebanese eggplant	3 lemons	Camomile tea
5 celery sticks	½ lime	Peppermint tea
8 asparagus spears	2 serves of fruit	Lemon tea
1 eggplant		2 cups basmati rice
1½ avocado	**Seafood**	800g (28 oz) canned
¼ yellow capsicum	100g (3½ oz) smoked	chickpeas
1¼ red capsicum	salmon	Sea salt
1 Lebanese cucumber	2 white fish fillets	Black pepper
1 bunch broccolini		250ml (1 cup) olive
1½ cups wom bok	**Dairy case**	oil
1 cup bean shoots	6 serves of cheese	23 eggs
4 sun-dried tomatoes	½ cup cream	250g (9 oz) frozen
1 onion	7 tblsp Parmesan	spinach
2 white onions	cheese	¼ tsp nutmeg
12 spring onions	5 tblsp sour cream	350g (12 oz) canned
2 red onions	200g (7 oz) ricotta	asparagus
½ long red chilli	75g (2½ oz) blue vein	¼ tsp ground
1½ birds-eye chillies	cheese	coriander
6 garlic cloves	6 tblsp butter	3 bay leaves
6 large radicchio	100g (3½ oz) feta	10 black peppercorns
leaves	2 triangles	½ tsp chilli powder
½ iceberg lettuce	kefalograviera	1½ tblsp oregano
3 cups rocket		1 tblsp thyme
1 cup baby spinach		2 tsp paprika
leaves		2 tblsp tomato paste
2 cups parsley		¼ tsp sambal oelek
2½ tblsp mint		1 tsp cumin
1 tblsp chives		½ tsp turmeric
½ cup dill		
4 stems rosemary		
2 tblsp Vietnamese		
mint		
½ cup coriander		
½ tblsp oregano		

NB: Substitute fresh herbs with dried herbs, if desired, where appropriate.

Week 2 preparation and cooking

Vegetable stock: Use this for *Vegetable risotto* and for *Asparagus soup*.

Vegetable risotto: This recipe makes enough for 2 people for 2 meals each.

Chickpea dip: Halve this recipe to make enough dip for 2 people for 2 servings each with *Vegetable crudités*.

Spinach and Parmesan cheese bake with ricotta and blue vein cheese: This recipes makes enough for 2 people for 2 servings each.

Asparagus soup: This recipe makes enough for 2 people for 2 servings each.

Day 8

Breakfast (Carbohydrate)

- *Muesli with apricots, mandarin and vanilla.* Serve with malt-free soymilk and top with diced peaches in natural juice
- Beverage suggestion – 1 cup of decaffeinated, or 97% caffeine-free, tea with optional malt-free soymilk

Lunch (Carbohydrate)

- *Vegetable risotto*
- Beverage suggestion – 1 cup of decaffeinated, or 97% caffeine-free, tea with optional malt-free soymilk
- Beverage suggestion – 1 glass of water

Snack (Carbohydrate)

- *Vegetable crudités* with *Chickpea dip*
- Beverage suggestion – 1 glass of water

Wait at least three hours after your snack before eating dinner

Dinner (Protein)

- *Zucchini and smoked salmon frittata with snipped chives and fresh dill*
- Beverage suggestion – 1 cup of camomile tea
- Beverage suggestion – 1 glass of water

Day 9

Breakfast (Carbohydrate)

- *Muesli with apricots, mandarin and vanilla.* Serve with malt-free soymilk and top with diced apricots in natural juice
- Beverage suggestion – 1 cup of decaffeinated, or 97% caffeine-free, tea with optional malt-free soymilk

Wait at least three hours after breakfast before eating lunch

Lunch (Protein)

- *Spinach and Parmesan ckeese bake with ricotta and blue vein cheese*
- Beverage suggestion – 1 cup of camomile tea
- Beverage suggestion – 1 glass of water

Snack (Protein)

- Serve of cheese
- Beverage suggestion – 1 glass of water

Dinner (Protein)

- *Asparagus soup*
- Beverage suggestion – 1 cup of peppermint tea
- Beverage suggestion – 1 glass of water

Day 10

Breakfast (Carbohydrate)

- *Muesli with apricots, mandarin and vanilla.* Serve with malt-free soymilk and top with diced pears in natural juice
- Beverage suggestion – 1 cup of decaffeinated, or 97% caffeine-free, tea with optional malt-free soymilk

Lunch (Carbohydrate)

- *Vegetable risotto*
- Beverage suggestion – 1 cup of decaffeinated, or 97% caffeine-free, tea with optional malt-free soymilk
- Beverage suggestion – 1 glass of water

Snack (Carbohydrate)

- *Vegetable crudités* with *Chickpea dip*
- Beverage suggestion – 1 glass of water

Wait at least three hours after your snack before eating dinner

Dinner (Protein)

- *Spicy fish fillets with tomato salsa served with garlic and chilli broccolini*
- Beverage suggestion – 1 cup of camomile tea
- Beverage suggestion – 1 glass of water

Day 11

Breakfast (Carbohydrate)

- *Muesli with apricots, mandarin and vanilla.* Serve with malt-free soymilk and top with diced peaches in natural juice
- Beverage suggestion – 1 cup of decaffeinated, or 97% caffeine-free, tea with optional malt-free soymilk

Wait at least three hours after breakfast before eating lunch

Lunch (Protein)

- *Spinach and Parmesan cheese bake with ricotta and blue vein cheese*
- Beverage suggestion – 1 cup of camomile tea
- Beverage suggestion – 1 glass of water

Snack (Protein)

- Serve of cheese
- Beverage suggestion – 1 glass of water

Dinner (Protein)

- *Vegetarian san choy bow*
- Beverage suggestion – 1 cup of camomile tea
- Beverage suggestion – 1 glass of water

Day 12

Breakfast (Carbohydrate)

- *Muesli with apricots, mandarin and vanilla.* Serve with malt-free soymilk and top with diced pears in natural juice
- Beverage suggestion – 1 cup of decaffeinated, or 97% caffeine-free, tea with optional malt-free soymilk

Lunch (Carbohydrate)

- *Chickpea salad*
- Beverage suggestion – 1 cup of decaffeinated, or 97% caffeine-free, tea with optional malt-free soymilk
- Beverage suggestion – 1 glass of water

Snack (Carbohydrate)

- Serve of fruit
- Beverage suggestion – 1 glass of water

Wait at least three hours after your snack before eating dinner

Dinner (Protein)

- *Asparagus soup*
- Beverage suggestion – 1 cup of camomile tea
- Beverage suggestion – 1 glass of water

Day 13

Breakfast (Protein)

- *Omelette with salmon, sour cream and fresh chives*
- Beverage suggestion – 1 cup of peppermint tea

Lunch (Protein)

- *Radicchio and feta rolls*
- Beverage suggestion – 1 cup of peppermint tea
- Beverage suggestion – 1 glass of water

Snack (Protein)

- Serve of cheese
- Beverage suggestion – 1 glass of water

Dinner (Protein)

- *Vegetable kebabs with Cajun spices and spicy tomato salsa*
- Beverage suggestion – 1 cup of camomile tea
- Beverage suggestion – 1 glass of water

Day 14

Breakfast (Protein)

- *Saganaki served with rocket*
- Beverage suggestion – 1 cup of camomile tea

Lunch (Protein)

- *Egg roll-ups*
- Beverage suggestion – 1 cup of peppermint tea
- Beverage suggestion – 1 glass of water

Snack (Protein)

- *Vegetable crudités*
- Beverage suggestion – 1 glass of water

Dinner (Protein)

- *Avocado and tomato salsa with barbecued vegetables*
- Beverage suggestion – 1 cup of lemon tea
- Beverage suggestion – 1 glass of water

Week 3 shopping

Vegetables	Fruit	Grocery
2 white onions	4 x 140g (4½ oz) punnet diced peaches in natural juice	700g (23 oz) rolled oats
10 spring onions		100g (3½ oz) processed bran
2½ brown onions		60g (2 oz) coarse oatmeal
3 garlic cloves	4 x 140g (4½ oz) punnet diced pears in natural juice	200g (7 oz) diced apricots
6 celery sticks		
4 tomatoes		3 litres (8 cups) malt-free soymilk
6 Roma tomatoes	4 x 140g (4½ oz) punnet diced apricots in natural juice	Decaffeinated tea
12 grape tomatoes		Camomile tea
350g (12 oz) green beans		Peppermint tea
10 asparagus spears	6 serves of fruit	Lemon tea
3 baby yellow squash	1 lemon	800g (28 oz) canned diced tomatoes
25 button mushrooms	½ lime	
100g (3½ oz) mixed mushrooms		400g (14 oz) can kidney beans
3 oyster mushrooms	**Seafood**	2 tblsp tomato paste
½ red capsicum	100g (3½ oz) smoked salmon	Sea salt
½ zucchini		Black pepper
½ fennel	2 fish fillets	3 bay leaves
½ eggplant	150g (5 oz) large uncooked prawns	10 peppercorns
1 broccoli		200ml (¾ cup) olive oil
4 baby bok choy		
½ birds-eye chilli	**Dairy case**	16 eggs
½ tsp ginger	2 cups fresh spiral pasta	1 tblsp baby capers
2 kaffir lime leaves		250g (9 oz) frozen spinach
6 large raddichio leaves	5 tblsp cream	
	1 cup grated cheese	¼ tsp nutmeg
1 cup baby spinach leaves	1 cup Parmesan cheese	1 tblsp white wine vinegar
2½ tblsp oregano	5 tblsp butter	½ tsp cumin
2½ cups parsley	750g (26 oz) ricotta	½ tsp paprika
4 stems rosemary	100g (3½ oz) feta	Dash chilli pepper
1 tblsp tarragon	2 serves of cheese	400g (14 oz) canned chickpeas
12 basil leaves		6 saffron threads
½ cup coriander		½ cup Doongara or basmati rice
½ cup Thai basil		3 tblsp peanut oil
		1½ tsp sesame oil
		1 tblsp almond slivers
		1 tsp fish sauce

NB: Substitute fresh herbs with dried herbs, if desired, where appropriate.

Week 3 preparation and cooking

Vegetable stock: Use to make *Quick minestrone*. Freeze any remaining stock.

Spinach roulade with mushroom and cheese filling: This recipe makes enough for 2 people for 2 servings each.

Smoked salmon dip: This recipe makes enough dip for 2 people for 3 servings each with *Vegetable crudités*.

Vegetarian omelette: This recipe makes enough for 2 people for 2 servings each.

Quick minestrone: This recipe makes enough soup for 2 people for 2 servings each.

Baked ricotta tarts with roast tomatoes and basil: This recipe makes enough for 2 people for 2 servings each.

Day 15

Breakfast (Carbohydrate)

- *Muesli with apricots, mandarin and vanilla.* Serve with malt-free soymilk and top with diced peaches in natural juice
- Beverage suggestion – 1 cup of decaffeinated, or 97% caffeine-free, tea with optional malt-free soymilk

Lunch (Carbohydrate)

- *Quick minestrone*
- Beverage suggestion – 1 cup of decaffeinated, or 97% caffeine-free, tea with optional malt-free soymilk
- Beverage suggestion – 1 glass of water

Snack (Carbohydrate)

- Serve of fruit
- Beverage suggestion – 1 glass of water

Wait at least three hours after your snack before eating dinner

Dinner (Protein)

- *Vegetarian omelette*
- Beverage suggestion – 1 cup of camomile tea
- Beverage suggestion – 1 glass of water

Day 16

Breakfast (Carbohydrate)

- *Muesli with apricots, mandarin and vanilla.* Serve with malt-free soymilk and top with diced apricots in natural juice
- Beverage suggestion – 1 cup of decaffeinated, or 97% caffeine-free, tea with optional malt-free soymilk

Wait at least three hours after breakfast before eating lunch

Lunch (Protein)

- *Spinach roulade with mushroom and cheese filling*
- Beverage suggestion – 1 cup of peppermint tea
- Beverage suggestion – 1 glass of water

Snack (Protein)

- *Vegetable crudités* with *Smoked salmon dip*
- Beverage suggestion – 1 glass of water

Dinner (Protein)

- *Grilled fish fillets with mixed vegetables*
- Beverage suggestion – 1 cup of camomile tea
- Beverage suggestion – 1 glass of water

Day 17

Breakfast (Carbohydrate)

- *Muesli with apricots, mandarin and vanilla*. Serve with malt-free soymilk and top with diced pears in natural juice
- Beverage suggestion – 1 cup of decaffeinated, or 97% caffeine-free, tea with optional malt-free soymilk

Lunch (Carbohydrate)

- *Quick minestrone*
- Beverage suggestion – 1 cup of decaffeinated, or 97% caffeine-free, tea with optional malt-free soymilk
- Beverage suggestion – 1 glass of water

Snack (Carbohydrate)

- Serve of fruit
- Beverage suggestion – 1 glass of water

Wait at least three hours after your snack before eating dinner

Dinner (Protein)

- *Baked ricotta tarts with roast tomatoes and basil*
- Beverage suggestion – 1 cup of camomile tea
- Beverage suggestion – 1 glass of water

Day 18

Breakfast (Carbohydrate)

- *Muesli with apricots, mandarin and vanilla.* Serve with malt-free soymilk and top with diced peaches in natural juice
- Beverage suggestion – 1 cup of decaffeinated, or 97% caffeine-free, tea with optional malt-free soymilk

Wait at least three hours after breakfast before eating lunch

Lunch (Protein)

- *Spinach roulade with mushroom and cheese filling*
- Beverage suggestion – 1 cup of camomile tea
- Beverage suggestion – 1 glass of water

Snack (Protein)

- *Vegetable crudités* with *Smoked salmon dip*
- Beverage suggestion – 1 glass of water

Dinner (Protein)

- *Vegetable stir-fry*
- Beverage suggestion – 1 cup of camomile tea
- Beverage suggestion – 1 glass of water

Day 19

Breakfast (Carbohydrate)

- *Muesli with apricots, mandarin and vanilla.* Serve with malt-free soymilk and top with diced pears in natural juice
- Beverage suggestion – 1 cup of decaffeinated, or 97% caffeine-free, tea with optional malt-free soymilk

Lunch (Carbohydrate)

- *Spicy tomato and chickpeas with saffron-flavoured doongara rice*
- Beverage suggestion – 1 cup of decaffeinated, or 97% caffeine-free, tea with optional malt-free soymilk
- Beverage suggestion – 1 glass of water

Snack (Carbohydrate)

- Serve of fruit
- Beverage suggestion – 1 glass of water

Wait at least three hours after your snack before eating dinner

Dinner (Protein)

- *Vegetarian omelette*
- Beverage suggestion – 1 cup of camomile tea
- Beverage suggestion – 1 glass of water

Day 20

Breakfast (Carbohydrate)

- *Muesli with apricots, mandarin and vanilla.* Serve with malt-free soymilk and top with diced apricots in natural juice
- Beverage suggestion – 1 cup of decaffeinated, or 97% caffeine-free, tea with optional malt-free soymilk

Wait at least three hours after breakfast before eating lunch

Lunch (Protein)

- *Baked ricotta tarts with roast tomatoes and basil*
- Beverage suggestion – 1 cup of peppermint tea
- Beverage suggestion – 1 glass of water

Snack (Protein)

- *Vegetable crudités* with *Salmon dip*
- Beverage suggestion – 1 glass of water

Dinner (Protein)

- *Asian-style braised vegetables*
- Beverage suggestion – 1 cup of lemon tea
- Beverage suggestion – 1 glass of water

Day 21

Breakfast (Protein)

- *Mixed mushroom omelette*
- Beverage suggestion – 1 cup of camomile tea

Lunch (Protein)

- *Radicchio and feta rolls*
- Beverage suggestion – 1 cup of lemon tea
- Beverage suggestion – 1 glass of water

Snack (Protein)

- Serve of cheese
- Beverage suggestion – 1 glass of water

Dinner (Protein)

- *Stir-fried prawns, beans and bok choy with ginger and kaffir lime leaves*
- Beverage suggestion – 1 cup of peppermint tea
- Beverage suggestion – 1 glass of water

Glossary

Bok choy: Chinese green leafy vegetable, similar to spinach

Broccolini: Italian broccoli-like vegetable

Capsicum: bell pepper

Chickpeas: garbanzo beans

Choy Sum: Chinese broccoli

Coriander: cilantro

Eggplant: aubergine

Fennel bulb: bulb-like white vegetable, smells like aniseed

Flat-leaf parsley: Italian or Continental parsley

Gruyere cheese: Swiss fondue cheese

Haloumi: Greek-style cheese

Harissa: Middle Eastern spice mixture

Kaffir lime leaves: Thai double-lobed citrus leaves

Kefalograviera: Greek-style cheese

Mince meat: ground meat

Prawns: shrimp

Raddicchio: red-coloured lettuce variety

Saffron threads: Indian spice

Spring onion: shallot, green onion

Sumac: Middle Eastern dried lemon flavoured berries

Tamarind puree: made from the fruit of the tamarind tree

Wom bok: Chinese cabbage

Zucchini: courgette

Weights and Measures

Dry weights

30g = 1 oz
60g = 2 oz
90g = 3 oz
125g = 4 oz
150g = 5 oz
200g = 7 oz
250g = 8 oz
315g = 10 oz
500g = 16 oz (1lb)
1kg = 32 oz (2 lb)

Liquid measures

30ml = 1 fl oz
60ml = 2 fl oz
90ml = 3 fl oz
125ml = 4 fl oz
150ml = 5 fl oz
200ml = 7 fl oz
250ml = 8 fl oz
300ml = 10 fl oz
500ml = 16 fl oz
600ml = 20 fl oz (1 pint)

1 cup = 250ml (8 fl oz)
1 tablespoon = 20ml (4 teaspoons)

Cooking temperatures

very slow	120°C	250°F
slow	150°C	200°F
moderately slow	160°C	315°F
moderate	180°C	350°F
moderately hot	200°C	400°F
hot	220°C	425°F
very hot	240°C	475°F

Recipe Index

Risotto with basmati rice, spinach and mixed herbs   64

Vegetable risotto   135

Salads

Asian prawn salad with chilli and lime dressing   127

Burghul and chickpea salad with mandarins   123

Burghul salad with sun-dried tomatoes, cucumber, parsley and mint   148

Cajun spiced basmati rice salad with tomatoes, red kidney beans and fresh herbs   117

Chicken Caesar salad   45

Chickpea salad   153

Chilli octopus and calamari salad   60

Feta, sun-dried tomatoes and prosciutto rolls with rocket salad   118

Grilled haloumi, tomato and eggplant salad   146

Lamb salad with lemon dressing   173

Lentil salad with chilli, capsicum and celery   150

Pepper beef and blue cheese salad with fresh parsley and chive dressing   48

Radicchio and rocket salad with cherry tomatoes, prosciutto and Parmesan cheese   122

Salad with sumac   119

Sashimi salmon salad with wasabi and lime dressing   106

Tuna, bean and egg salad   76

Seafood

Barbecued prawns with basil, chilli and kaffir lime leaves served with an Asian salad   90

Barramundi fillets with Thai flavours   158

Crab and prawn cakes with chilli and ginger served with chilli and lime dressing   94

Fish fillets with walnut and lemon, served with squash and asparagus stir-fry   174

Fish fillets wrapped in vine leaves with saffron, leeks and parsley   116

Grilled fish fillets with mixed vegetables   74

Grilled mussel omelette with parsley   104

Prawn and pork skewers with rosemary and anchovy marinade   156

Salmon steaks served on asparagus with fresh dill dressing   33

Sardines and tomatoes with caper and parsley dressing   46

Sardines wrapped in vine leaves with spiced garlic and almond butter served with fennel, tomato and parsley salad   181

Skewered prawns served with Greek salad   101

Smoked salmon, caper, tarragon and dill muffins   125

Snapper with chilli and lime served with spinach and cucumber salad   167

Spicy fish fillets with tomato salsa served with garlic and chilli broccolini   49

Spicy roasted baby snapper with garlic and sage spinach   43

Stir-fried prawns, beans and bok choy with ginger and kaffir lime leaves   36

Stir-fried spicy octopus served with avocado salsa   165

For all enquiries including updates, recipes, support services and ordering any of our books and products, please go to the following website address:

www.glycemic-index.com

Orders can also be made through the following address:

Better Healing Solutions
PO Box 5207
Burnley, Vic 3121

Ph: 1300 137 014